D068875I

FASHION
The Changing Shape of Fashion
Through the Years

This page:
Edwardian bathing costumes,
1910.

Title page:
Charles II dancing at The
Hague, by Hieronymus
Janssens.

Contents page:
Silhouette of the Cramsie
Family, 18th century.

Front endpaper:
Hunting tapestry showing a
boar and bear hunt.

Back endpaper:
Dresses designed by John
Bates.

FASHION

The Changing Shape of Fashion Through the Years

JANE DORNER

With a Foreword by

ELIZABETH ANN COLEMAN

Curator, Costume & Textile Department,
The Brooklyn Museum, New York

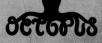

First published 1974 by
Octopus Books Limited
59 Grosvenor Street, London W1

ISBN 0 7064 0344 4

© 1974 Octopus Books Limited

Produced by Mandarin Publishers Limited
14 Westlands Road Quarry Bay Hong Kong
Printed in Hong Kong

Distributed in USA by
Crescent Books
a division of Crown Publishers Inc
419 Park Avenue South
New York N.Y. 10016

Distributed in Australia by
Rigby Limited
30 North Terrace, Kent Town
Adelaide, South Australia 5067

Contents

Foreword 7

Introduction 9

1 Fashion before 1700 11

2 A Woman's Shape 1700-1970s 27

3 Conscious Display 47

4 Trousers and Sports Clothes 67

5 Dandies and Spivs 83

6 American Influences 99

7 Postscript – Couture and After

Index 127
Bibliographical Acknowledgments 128
Picture Acknowledgments 128

Foreword

Ever since that day when mankind first fashioned a self covering, comments on garments, either derogatory or complimentary, seem to have flown fast and furiously. For few things in life are more subjective than our choice in the matter of personal adornment and in our interpretation of what others wear or have worn. No one, perhaps, has expressed the opinion more succinctly than the Scot, Robert Burns, when he wrote in 'To a Louse':

O wad some Pow'r the giftie gie us
To see oursels as ithers see us!
It wad frae monie a blunder free us
And foolish notion.

At the moment there is the question of how we view the radical change in the dressing style of members of the opposite sex. For the first time in nearly two hundred years the male is assuming a multi-coloured, multi-patterned, perfumed and powdered appearance. The female, it would seem, has almost traded her appearance for his by accepting the stark linear façade provided by both the mini skirt and the pantsuit. Current analysers of trends will proclaim that the more utilitarian 'pants outfits' on women have been brought about by 'emancipation'; but are they more emancipated because they sit behind a desk or stand in a factory assembly line than if they manage the household chores or work on a farm. In reality female emancipation means freedom of choice – at the ballot box, in selection of occupation, etc. And women have chosen the trousered outfits of men as being the most practical to their assorted endeavours. However, if the Scottish kilt had been the accepted twentieth century male attire, one can be sure that the female, had she been in trousers, would have adopted the skirt as her challenging mode of dress.

Changing concepts of beauty are at work just as much as the desire to be free from constraining raiment. Pacesetters in taste issue dicta as much from boredom and economic needs as from aesthetic considerations. An outfit of 1960 looks downright ugly to our eyes today because we have been taught to appreciate a new set of lines and a different colour palette. The garment of 1950 looks 'funny' in a nostalgic way, while those of 1940 have reached that age where they have passed into the revival stage. That is, those who originally wore the outfits consider them still hideously ugly but there is a new generation that dares to interpret the outfits of its immediate predecessors' youth. The resulting 'look' is a bastardization, as it is based more on contemporary taste than on historical fact.

It is commonly accepted by costume historians that the basic influencing factors in the development of styles have been, and I list at random: climate, technological advances, sexual display, political, social and economic structures, historical precedent and more recently the mass media. Yet, even in an age of almost instant communications it is still possible for even a non fashion-con-

Opposite: Venetian courtesans by Carpaccio c. 1465 The picture shows all the accessories of wealthy ladies of leisure – clean white handkerchief, the extra high shoes, the ornamental dog, plenty of jewelry and the slashed sleeves.

Below: Greek drapery, on which much of 14th century costume was based.

Below: Marie Antoinette initiated a craze for high-born ladies dressing as peasant girls. She is seen here at the Petit Trianon with a lady-in-waiting in court dress, in an engraving romanticized by a 19th century artist.

scious traveller to note that styles in the world's great metropolitan centres differ more from their outlying areas than they do from each other. Why, one may ask? One of the multiheaded answers may be that the cities provide a habitat for experimentalists, devotees of traditional crafts, the affluent, the taste-setters, and an international market place. All this works out as a laboratory where the

most common denominator garment is evolved for transmittal to suburban areas. A ride on the New York City subway system between Harlem, the upper East Side and Greenwich Village shows this process in action, for the riders are arrayed in extremes first espoused by those enclaves as well as modified versions of garments worn earlier in these three diametrically opposed fashion centres of New York. From city centre the fashions will move in to the surrounding countryside in a substantially diluted form that is accepted as current fashion for a longer period than it initially was in the urban area. In undergoing its rigorous testing a 'look' can be said to be going from fad to fashion to style. The cut of garments may vary little from continent to

continent in the urban areas but nations stand apart in terms of colour and the texture of their fabrics. Taking a person from head to toe it is still possible to tell whether he or she is French, British, Italian, American or what have you, because even more than the basic body covering accessories such as shoes, eyeglasses, handbags, or the mode of hairdressing will give clues to a national origin.

Our image of ourselves and of our ancestors is most highly coloured by interpretations made in the written analyses of current fashion reporters and by fashion historians. And each of these in turn is influenced by the currently accepted modes of thought. Thus, in the nineteenth century, fashions in garments as well as in the decorative arts and architecture were explained in terms of their supposedly relevant historical derivation: i.e. a bodice 'à la Sévigné'. In the twentieth century, with seemingly more relaxed moral standards, practically all modes of attire are discussed in terms of their sexual meaning. In both forms of interpretation time will see them out-moded and a new explanative vogue will come.

In compiling a history of fashion, whatever its point of view, the author must face the inclusion of generalities. Perhaps such treatment is more valid in writing on fashion and taste than in other areas. In this book, Jane Dorner has selected a most telling quotation from the eighteenth-century Austrian Empress, Maria Theresa: 'I was always of the opinion that one should follow the fashions with restraint but never exaggerate them.' Two hundred years later the majority of fashion-conscious people follow her precepts.

Elizabeth Ann Coleman

Introduction

This book concentrates on the period from 1700 to the present day, which may, in broad historical terms, be called the modern period. All the threads of fashion running through the earlier centuries – the underlying themes and assumptions that have produced the changing styles and shapes – are seen to be interwoven in the last three, with the present century marking a complete change towards the democratization of fashion.

Eighteenth-century styles reveal a continuation of the love of splendour that had been apparent since the fourteenth century, for the elaborate finery of the court distinguished them from the lower orders in a way that matched the snobbery of the era. Nineteenth-century clothes reflect a period of innovation in social attitudes, and fashions changed more often than they had in all the previous five centuries. This constant variety was due in some measure to the fact that fashions were becoming available to a wider range of people, with the result that the upper classes were constantly seeking novelty in a bid to retain their social superiority. Children, who were generally considered by the leisured classes as mere decorative appendages, were dressed as miniature adults and were not freed completely from constricting clothes until the twentieth century (though this process had begun at the end of the eighteenth century). Today the tendency towards freedom and equality among all classes has gradually increased, so that it is now barely possible to distinguish a duchess from her domestic by their daily dress.

The book concentrates on fashions in Britain, France and the United States of America, since these three countries have had, or are having, the greatest influence on the western fashion scene. Throughout the centuries innumerable styles have originated in the fashion capitals, and only those details that relate to the main themes of the book have been picked out: costume that asserts class distinction, the phenomenon of sexual display, decorative dandyism, physical freedom, social equality and self-expression.

Below: A citizen's wife, a countrywoman and a countryman, from John Speed's map 'The Empire of Great Britain', 1605.

Following page: The marriage of Edward II of England to Isabella of France in Boulogne in 1308. From Froissart's Chronicles, painted in the early 15th century. The ladies in the royal retinue are wearing the steeple head-dresses of the time.

9

Chapter One

Fashion Before 1700

Sewing the threads

Both Plato and Sir Thomas More, when considering the organization of an ideal state, turned their attention to the important matter of clothing. Those serious-minded sages would have had us all dress the same, in a toga-like garment of plain, undecorated, durable cloth. By recognizing the need for control they acknowledged the fact that human beings, left to themselves, will dress to achieve a variety of aims – chiefly to flaunt or disguise the ego, or to emphasize the distinctions based on sex, breeding and wealth that the simple Utopian life would eliminate. Fortunately for the art of costume, however, the social structure (of the western world at least) has always depended on these distinctions. At each stage in its evolution the individual has been able to define his position within society by certain external signs, of which dress is one of the most significant. The outward form is so often taken for the thing itself that the individual who wishes to step out of his social sphere into the one above will adopt the dress of that new class as much as its attitudes. By dressing like a lady a woman hopes to be accepted as one, while the true lady will then advance the dictates of fashion to a pitch where the common aspirant cannot hope to follow. It is this continual upward movement of the individual's social ambitions that has been responsible for the variety of fashion shapes in the western world, particularly in the last two and a half centuries. By con-

trast, in China and Japan, where the social structure was rigid and outside influences were discouraged, costume remained fundamentally unchanged for about a thousand years.

It is tempting to think that the innumerable styles that costume has assumed at different times have been no more than random searchings for something new; in fact there has almost always been some idea, deliberate or instinctive, behind the fashions, whether they are designed to express class distinctions, to display male virility or female intangibility, to flaunt frivolity, to convey the repressions of prudery or, conversely, freedom from constraint. Clothes have always been outward manifestations of prevailing social attitudes: they represent morals pictorially, and their various aspects represent the threads of fashion from which the total silhouette is sewn.

Before following these strands, in what may broadly be called the modern period of fashion, it is necessary to thread the needle, as it were, and go back to the point at which fashion may be said to have begun.

Body coverings have, of course, been worn since prehistoric cavemen first felt a need for extra warmth and flung over their bodies the skins of the animals they slew for meat. The invention of spinning and weaving led to more comfortable wear and the decoration of simple garments grew in complexity as civilization advanced, until a point was reached when different colours or pat-

Below: Japanese courtly dress showed the same signs of inconvenience as European courtly dress. Note the shoes that are too high and the trousers which are half as long again as the height of the man, in this Japanese silk painting, 19th century.

Right: Peasants wearing cotehardies, coloured tights and cowls from the Luttrell Psalter, c. 1340. The cotehardie was practical, allowing plenty of room for movement in the skirt.

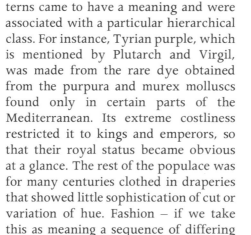

Right: Peasants wearing cotehardies, coloured tights and cowls from the Luttrell Psalter, c. 1340. The cotehardie was practical, allowing plenty of room for movement in the skirt.

Below: A 14th century French ivory depicting an attack on the Castle of Love shows armour and women's costume of the time. The ladies wear loose kirtles and the head-dresses have templers over the ears.

terns came to have a meaning and were associated with a particular hierarchical class. For instance, Tyrian purple, which is mentioned by Plutarch and Virgil, was made from the rare dye obtained from the purpura and murex molluscs found only in certain parts of the Mediterranean. Its extreme costliness restricted it to kings and emperors, so that their royal status became obvious at a glance. The rest of the populace was for many centuries clothed in draperies that showed little sophistication of cut or variation of hue. Fashion – if we take this as meaning a sequence of differing shapes of garments – does not really begin until the art of fitting a garment to the shape of the body had been acquired. We can regard this art as beginning in the middle of the fourteenth century.

The Age of Chivalry (1350-1485)

The typical garment of the Dark Ages was a loose-fitting tunic worn by both men and women. Labourers and villeins wore a shortened version, tied at the waist with a girdle. Changes came slowly, but as ladies cast their civilizing influence over court and castle and became glamorized in the institution of courtly love, so their dress became closer-fitting, more alluring and revealing. Even the modest damsel uncovered her bosom a little, and wore a kirtle or gown that hugged her closely at the waist and then flared out in long, full folds, while tight-fitting sleeves emphasized her slender figure. But the married woman's greatest attraction – her hair – was kept alluringly hidden beneath a series of fantastic head-dresses that grew increasingly elaborate as the fourteenth and fifteenth centuries advanced.

These head-dresses find their parallel later in the wigs of the eighteenth century, which acted as posters for advertising a woman's importance. Sometimes the actual hair was used as an ingredient in the general structure, with plaits over the ears forming the basis of the square face framing that was so popular in the late fourteenth century. These plaits or coils of hair were enclosed in a *crespine*, or net, and were known as templers. Their combined width occasionally measured as much as twice that of the face. In the early fifteenth century a horned structure, the hennin, was added, made up of

covered padding in the shape of cow's horns with veils falling down at the back, and another popular style was the heart-shaped head-dress.

Extra height, a recurrent thread in the history of fashion, was gained by the steeple head-dress, which took the form of a truncated cone from which hung ribbons and gauzes. It was never very tall in England, but it reached absurd heights in Germany and France, where it echoed the soaring lines of Gothic architecture. But perhaps the most spectacular structure of the fifteenth century was the butterfly head-dress, which was popular in England until about 1485, when the changes effected by the house of Tudor altered the tide of fashion. It was a wire structure rising high above the head and supporting a diaphanous veil in the shape of a butterfly's wings, an embroidered cap holding the hair in place beneath it. These head-dresses seem to represent the first real items of gratuitous display in women's dress, since they required care in manipulation and demanded hours of patient making and fitting.

For the knight, with his elegant ideals of chivalry and courtesy, clothes had a dual function – to allow him to cut a good figure in the eyes of his adored mistress and to decorate the field of battle. Tournaments, an essential part of knightly training, were gorgeous affairs with men dressed up in their most colourful attire. Bright scarlet gowns of velvet and satin intermingled with blues and greens, lined with cloth of gold tissue and trimmed with fur, presented a vivid kaleidoscope. A lively effect of movement was achieved by the flowing sleeves with jagged, leaf-shaped or otherwise dagged edges, which displayed a lining of a different colour from the rest of the costume.

Heraldic devices were embroidered in rich silks on the clothes of men and women alike to demonstrate their lineage to friend or foe. The lower orders, who could boast of no decorative quarterings, were nevertheless attracted by the gala of colour and copied where they could, until sumptuary laws put a stop to what their pockets must otherwise have prevented. Laws enacted during the reign of the English king Edward III made quite explicit the fact that a man could decorate his person only according to his status:

All esquires and every gentleman under the estate of knighthood, and not possessed of lands or tenements to the yearly amount of 200 marks, shall use in their dress such cloth as does not exceed the value of 4 marks and a half the whole cloth; they shall not wear any cloth of gold, of silk, or of silver, nor any sort of embroidered garment, nor any ring, buckle, nouche, riband nor girdle; nor any ornaments of precious stones, nor furs of any kind; their wives and children shall be subject to the same regulations.

The simple folk had to be content with homespun cloth such as fustian – a twilled mixture of cotton and linen–and sackcloth of natural hodden grey or dyed with cheap dyes such as russet and indigo. Privilege came with status, the merchant, for example, being allowed a long robe bordered with fur to accentuate his dignity, though even then he was restricted to fox, coney or cat fur. The illustrations to Chaucer's *Canterbury Tales* from the Ellesmere Manuscript of about 1400 indicate more eloquently than words the differences in clothing between people at various levels of the social scale, and his parson expresses a common attitude to the wasteful expense of rich men's clothes:

On the one hand is the sin of extravagance in clothing, which is of harm to the people because it is so costly. There is not only the expense of the embroidery with its elaborate heraldic designs of zig-zags, bars, waves, stripes, vertical or horizontal bands, and suchlike wastefulness of material through

Above: The popular butterfly head-dress is seen on this brass rubbing of Anne Herward, 1485, from a church in Norfolk.

Below: The Ellesmere manuscript dated c. 1400 is one of the most beautifully illustrated versions of Chaucer's Canterbury Tales. Seen here are the knight and the wife of Bath.

vanity; but there is also the expense of the fur linings for their gowns.... On the other hand is the sin of a disgusting and inordinant scantiness in clothing in such garments as smocks and jackets which are so short that they do not cover a man's shameful members, which leads to wicked designs....

The revealing tightness of the hose and near-nakedness across the buttocks shocked the clerics, as did some of the other absurdities of men's dress, such as fanciful headgear and, above all, pointed shoes that sometimes reached a toe length of 18 inches. These 'piked shoes', also called *crackowes* or *poulaines* after the town of Cracow in Poland where they are thought to have originated, seemingly, could be worn only by those who had no work to do, and indeed no need to walk anywhere. They are an early example of the relationship between inconvenience of dress and assertion of rank – an aspect of fashion that continues right down through the nineteenth century.

The Gorgeous Age (1485-1610)

The desire for decoration reached its peak in the slashed clothing that spread to the rest of Europe from Italy. An advantage was that it displayed to the world the wearer's ability to obtain undergarments of fine linen by cutting slits in the outer costume and pulling a contrasting colour through. (The custom was said to have originated with the mercenary soldiers who put good clothes under their rags in the late fifteenth century.) Sleeves and the front

Right and opposite: Hand-maidens representing the four parts of the Holy Roman Empire – Slavinia, Germania, Gaul and Rome – offer homage to Otto III, seen enthroned in the second picture. The costumes exhibit the typical Byzantine draperies of the 10th century. Taken from Reichenau's Gospel Book of Otto III.

Above: Henry VIII, attributed to Holbein, wearing an overgown heavily embroidered with gold thread.

Below: Two Holbein drawings depicting typical men and women's costume in the early 16th century.

of the doublet – a short padded jacket now universally worn with breeches and motley-coloured hose – lent themselves particularly well to this treatment, but as slashing became more popular other areas began to be exploited. The tops of the breeches were quite literally cut to ribbons in a variety of patterns, the slashings on one leg running in a different direction from those on the other. The German *Landsknecht* illustrates this fashion in its most extreme form, while the costume of the Swiss Guards at the Vatican today continues the tradition in a modified version.

Women's clothes afforded less scope for slashing, since only the sleeves were suitable for such treatment, so men lorded it as the peacocks of the fashion scene in the early sixteenth century. Women were encased in the type of superstructure disguising the natural shape of the body that so often appears as an ingredient in women's fashions in the modern period. Doublets would be stuffed with bombast or other suitable material and combined with wide puffed sleeves to add extra breadth to the figure. The effect created was one of imposing squareness, admirably illustrated in Holbein's celebrated portrait of Henry VIII. The codpiece (*cod* meaning bag) was an additional area for flamboyant display in a dress whose emphasis lay on masculine virility. Henry himself loved dazzling his courtiers with the splendour of his clothes and at his coronation wore a crimson velvet robe trimmed with ermine, over a doublet embroidered with diamonds, rubies, emeralds and pearls. In late sixteenth-century France, crimson was by law the colour of the nobility and edicts issued under Henri III restricted its use still further. Princes and princesses might array themselves entirely in this glorious colour, but nobles and their wives might wear only one crimson article in their dress, while lower down the social scale only a dull red was permitted. Laws such as these, which ran counter to the natural desires of social climbers, were often flouted, in spite of the fact that penalties could be high, both for the

wearer and for the tailor who made the forbidden garment.

Sumptuary laws in England under Elizabeth I were so difficult to enforce that they were relaxed for a time. The second half of the sixteenth century was a prosperous period and all classes attempted to express the exuberant mood of the age in their dress. The queen herself had a passion for rich clothes and her gowns were a riot of embroideries encrusted with precious gems depicting flowers, animals, symbolic eyes and ears, rainbows, flames and pillars. One of her petticoats – not an undergarment in the modern sense of the word but a skirt attached to the bodice – is described in the royal wardrobe accounts of 1600: 'Item, one peticoate of white satten, embrodered all over with Venice golde, silver, and silk of divers colours, with a verie faire border of pomegranetts, pyneapple trees frutidge, and the nine Muses, in the same border.'

The rage for ornamentation was widespread, in spite of the fact that the finest clothes could not be washed. Soap had begun to be made in London in 1524 but it was expensive and could not deal adequately when the fine silk embroideries that gallants insisted on having on their riding breeches in defiance of rain and mud. Laundry bills must have reached their peak when ruffs came into general use. The first were worn in France in about 1540, and they were adopted in England some ten years later. Initially they were modest frills (a natural development of the frill formed by the drawstrings that fastened men's shirts at the neck), but they became imposing structures at the courts of England, France and Spain. The French king Henri III wore a ruff rather more than one foot deep, which contained over 18 yards of linen, all neatly pleated and folded in place with an ironing stick heated in the fire. French ruffs were so inconvenient that one royal lady is said to have been obliged to use a spoon with a handle two feet long to eat her soup, though quite why this helped it is difficult to see. The devil she supped with was obviously the vanity of rank and fashion prevailing over good sense and manners.

In England ruffs were commonly a quarter of a yard wide and were open in front. When Mrs Dinghen, the wife of Queen Elizabeth's Dutch coachman, brought the art of starching to England in 1564, their stiff elaborateness increased. This lady made a fortune by taking pupils and charging them £5 a head to learn the secret of the white and yellow starches then in vogue. Additional stiffening was achieved with wire covered in silk or gold thread, which was inserted under the ruff as a support

Above left: Back of an embroidered jacket, about 1610-30. Worn over a full skirt, the neckline would be embellished with a stiff lace standing collar.

Above: An Elizabethan embroidered woman's hood and man's night cap, worked in black silk on linen. Both show the preoccupation with stylized flowers, particularly the tudor rose.

Below: François I of France, by Clouet, mid-16th century.

*Above: Ladies at the court of
Isabella of France (wife of
Charles VI) receive the book
of Christina de Pisan, from
a 15th century manuscript.
They are wearing the head-
dresses typical of the period,
the hennin with thin veils
floating at the back and the
popular butterfly head-dress.*

*Right: Lady and gentlemen
from a French version of The
Romance of the Rose, 1350.
The men are plainly dressed
in long tunics and in this
and the illustration opposite
the lady wears a head-dress
typical of the time.*

Above: Sir Geoffrey Luttrell arming for the wars. He is wearing a gilt bascinet and silver mail with plated elbows and gauntlets, poleyns and greaves on the front of the shin and gilt spurs. The ladies are wearing garments showing the Luttrell arms. From the Luttrell Psalter, dated 1340.

Left: Lady and gentleman in The Romance of the Rose, 1350. He is wearing the cotehardie with coloured hose and long pointed shoes and also a cowl, from which developed the fool's cap and bells. She is a long kirtle with tight-fitting sleeves.

Above: Margin drawing from John Speed's map 'The Empire of Great Britain', 1605, showing a lady wearing the wheel farthingale which was popular at the end of Elizabeth I's reign.

to lighten the weight of the mass of material. Men and women alike wore ruffs and the effect was one of *hauteur*, reflecting the proud etiquette of the day.

Rigidity was indeed the thread running through Elizabethan fashions, and the fashion moralist of the day, Philip Stubbes, condemned it. In *The Anatomie of Abuses*, published in 1585, he writes, 'Doublets are quilted, stuffed, bombasted and sewed, as they can neither work nor yet well play in them… some are of satin, taffeta, silk and gold.' Women's clothes grew more inconvenient as the sixteenth century advanced. The bodice would be stiffened with buckram, or sometimes with wood, which made bending impossible, and attached to it was a skirt that swelled out over a farthingale, a structure made from hoops of wire, wood or whalebone. The farthingale reached France from Spain in the 1530s and made its first appearance in England in 1545. Its origin is unclear. The word farthingale is a corruption of the old French *vertugale*, which either comes from the Spanish *verdugo*, meaning a rod, or originated in the French *vertu-gardien*, meaning 'custodian of virtue'. Whether the latter meaning indicates its real intention, or whether, like the nineteenth-century crinoline, it was designed to make women more noticeable, is uncertain. At first its shape was similar to that of the dome-shaped crinoline, but an uglier

version of it gained popularity in the 1580s. This was the wheel farthingale, which created the impression that the wearer was standing inside a wheel with her skirt attached to the outer rim and falling vertically to the ground. The majority of women above the labouring classes wore a version of the farthingale, though it had sometimes shrunk to a padded 'bum roll' that tilted the skirt up at the back. There was a universal longing for finery without reference to practical considerations. In Act IV, Scene III of Shakespeare's *The Taming of the Shrew*, Petruchio teasingly tempts Katharine:

Will we return unto thy father's house,
And revel it as bravely as the best,
With silken coats and caps and golden rings,
With ruffs and cuffs and farthingales and
  things;
With scarves and fans and double change of
  bravery,
With amber bracelets, beads and all this
  knavery.

Some gentlewomen like Kate worked their own embroidery; it was one of their few diversions and they learnt the art early in their lives. Stylized flowers, especially the Tudor rose, were the main motifs, and also birds, insects and to a lesser degree geometric patterns. As the Elizabethan Age matured, the exuberance of patterning and adornment in

Right: Ladies and gentlemen in a ballroom, of the court of Louis XIV, engraved by Abraham Bosse. c. 1640. The gentlemen wear wide lace collars, doublet and breeches trimmed with braid and boots with bucket tops, which were criticized by pamphleteers for their wastage.

clothes gave way to the sophisticated costume of the seventeenth century.

Long Locks and Lace (1610-1700)

It was Cardinal Richelieu in France who seriously attempted to call a halt to the reckless extravagance of court functions, at which nobles would grow jealous of each other's wealth and appear at fêtes, ballets, masquerades and banquets dressed in such gorgeous garments that they could hardly move for the weight of gems and heavy materials. When the boy king, Louis XIII, came to the throne in 1610, Richelieu was able to rule through the queen regent, Marie de Médicis. He put a stop to foreign imports, to stem the flow of gold into Italy and Belgium, where most of the finery came from. His edicts confirmed the revolution in women's fashions. The farthingale disappeared along with the elaborate ornaments and the skirt now fell in straight deep folds from a tight-basqued bodice. The ruff was replaced first by a plain lawn band and then by a more elaborate flat collar with pointed lace edging, matched by similar lace at the cuff. The white lace attractively set off the sombre plainness of the dress and it remained standard wear for the middle classes in England and France for several decades. The costume was at its most austere in Holland, where black was the predominant colour, whereas the French aristocracy favoured various shades of green and colours with fanciful names such as 'kiss-me-my-love', 'wasted time' or 'mortal sin'.

Men's costume exhibited more panache, for this was a period of quick tempers and a fierce sense of honour, when 'hearts were bold, and men were men'. To our modern eye, the fashions may seem effeminate, bedecked as they were with feathered plumes, ribbons, ruffles, rosettes and the same fine falling lace collar as women wore. Yet the general effect – with a sword or rapier dangling from a decorative sword belt – was one of martial swagger. The swash-buckling image was sealed by the fanciful boots worn throughout the first half of the seventeenth century. Long boots, sometimes reaching above the knee, were made of fine leather and decorated with fringed tops, ruffles and jewelled buckles. Some boots were turned up at the toe to such an extent that it was almost impossible to walk in them and the pamphleteers railed against the 'flapping boot tops of the rich', which 'wasted leather that would serve the barefooted poor'.

This garb developed into the dress of the cavalier in the England of Charles I, where the elegant strove to achieve the appearance of graceful ease and luxury. Everything about their clothes was soft and rich, eschewing all hard lines or sharp contrasts. The hair, too, was natural, worn in thick masses of curls

Above: Isaac Oliver's miniature of Richard Sackville, 1616, shows the earl in full court dress: embroidered doublet and trunk hose, stockings with decorated clocks, and a standing band collar edged with lace matching the doublet cuffs. He wears the Vandyck beard which was very popular in the reign of Charles I.

Left: A second engraving by Bosse shows ladies at table in the Palais Royal, Paris. Low-cut dresses with an ornament in the bosom were more popular than the wide ruff collar of the lady on the right.

The jousts of St. Ingilbert in France, from Froissart's Chronicle, (early 15th century) showing the armour and dress of the period. Some ladies are wearing 'favours', handkerchiefs which they presented to the knight of their choice.

Left: The Phoenix portrait of Elizabeth I by Nicholas Hilliard c. 1575. Elizabeth's love of finery is exhibited in this jewel-encrusted and embroidered robe.

Right: The Old Pretender (son of James II of England) and his sister in full court dress. She wears the fontanges head-dress initiated at the court of Louis XIV. Children were commonly dressed as miniature adults. Painting by Nicholas Largillière, 1695.

arranged carelessly about the shoulders. It was basically the hair that differentiated the Royalist from the Puritan during the Civil War, for although not all Puritans were as sober in dress as Oliver Cromwell would have liked, he more extreme did cut their hair short — hence the name 'roundhead' — and eliminate from their dress the more extreme forms of decoration. Staunch Puritans tended to wear plain brown or black woollens, neatened by freshly laundered collar bands and cuffs. The women wore caps and aprons. The eleven years of the Commonwealth thus show a hiatus in fashion, though this was amply compensated for when Charles II returned to the throne in 1660.

Right: An engraving of Nell Gwynne, the famous beauty and favourite of Charles II, after a painting by Lely. She wears a hairstyle popular in the 1660s, featuring a row of curls, arranged across the forehead and ringleted side locks.

Charles was tall, slim and elegantly handsome, a connoisseur of the pleasures of life. He had spent many years of his exile dallying at the court of Louis XIV and inevitably brought back with him to England the latest French modes. But rivalry had grown between him and the Sun King, based partly on his envy of the absolutism of the French monarchy compared with his much curtailed powers in England, and may have led him to attempt innovations to break the monotony of the French dictatorship of fashion. His most significant innovation was a calf-length coat, called the 'vest', which was in effect the forerunner of the uniform of the eighteenth-century gentleman. John Evelyn describes it in an entry in his *Diary* for 18 October 1666; 'It being the first time his Majesty put himself into the eastern fashion of vest, changing doublet, stiff collar, bands and cloak into a comely dress after the Persian mode, with girdles or straps, and shoestrings and garters into buckles, of which some are set with precious stones.' Louis, perhaps to show his superiority in matters of fashion, mocked Charles by putting his footmen into vests, which made Samuel Pepys 'mighty merry, it being an ingenious kind of affront'. Charles's attempts to become a leader of fashion were further hampered by his plain wife, Catherine of Braganza, who came to England in 1667, bringing with her the stiff farthingales of the Portuguese court and obstinately trying to enforce them in fashionable English circles. But Charles's more beautiful mistresses brushed aside these attempts and continued to display their easy and graceful charms in dresses with a lower *décolletage* than had previously been seen in England. Costumes were now as extravagant as they were alluring. Lady Chaworth, writing to her brother Lord Roos on 2 November 1676, says: 'Mighty bravery in clothes preparing for the queen's birthday, especially Mis Phraser, whose gowne is ermine upon velvet imbroidered with gold and lined with cloth of gold; 'twill come to £300, and frights Sir Carr Scroope, who is much in love with her, from marrying her, saying his estate will scarce maintaine her in clothes!' Even in today's values, £300 is a vast amount to spend on one outfit, and we later read of 'Mis Phraser' wearing a gown said to have cost £800!

Nevertheless, Louis XIV was the true dictator of European fashion in the late seventeenth century. His courtiers had to dress as he wished, and felt obliged to copy every whim or fancy that derived from some innovation of one of his mistresses. When the beautiful Mlle de Fontanges was in favour she found that her elaborately dressed hair had been blown into disorder during a hunting party, so she tied it up in a ribbon, letting the ends fall over her forehead. The king was so entranced that the *'fontange'* head-dress was soon adopted by the rest of the court, later spreading to England, where it was popular throughout the 1690s and continued through the first decade of the eighteenth century. The original style was elaborated until it came to be made of tiers of frills of stiff linen and lace built upon a foundation of wire called a *commode*. Even children wore it, as can be seen in the portrait of Louisa Maria Theresa Stuart. In intention it may be compared with the head-dresses of the fifteenth century and the high wigs of the late eighteenth century. Men, too, increased their height by wearing the long full-bottomed wigs initiated by Louis XIV, who raised the technique of making perukes or periwigs to a fine art. He had no less than 40 wigmakers in attendance at Versailles. So the first

strands had been woven for the wig mania that was to sweep through the eighteenth century.

The taste for appliquéd motifs of gold and silver brocade, for ribbons and bows and rich lace trimmings also originated at the court of Versailles, where the glories of the Baroque style were reflected in the design of the palace itself. The enormous prestige of the court of Versailles resulted all over Europe in a readiness to accept the superiority of France in matters of fashion. This superiority remained unquestioned until the second half of the twentieth century.

Below: A lutenist, beribboned in true cavalier style. His doublet is trimmed with rosettes and embroidered bands and his breeches are tied at the bottom with bows. The long, curly hair was typical of the period. Engraved by Abraham Bosse, c. 1646.

Chapter Two

A Woman's Shape 1700-1970s

Opposite: Jean-Baptiste Mallet: The Bouquet. *The gowns, with the waist in its normal place and a slight bustle, date from the 1780s.*

One of the basic fashion impulses in the eighteenth century, as it had been during the Renaissance, was the urge to appear gorgeously decked. For this artifice was needed and women in the 'modern' period have become past-masters of this craft. They have contrived in the course of the last ten generations to disguise their natural form in a variety of shapes, looking now like baskets of fruit, now like milk churns, spinning tops, inverted flowers, bells – and boys. A woman's fashionable shape has tended to conceal the real contours of her body while emphasizing some of its sexual characteristics and has therefore tended to change with fluctuations in sexual attitudes in society. Clothes worn in the period from 1700 to the present day thus reflect the gradual change from the frivolous embroidered garments of the eighteenth-century aristocracy to the sedate clothes of the respectable nineteenth-century citizen, culminating in the twentieth century with the comfortable and carefree outfits of the emancipated woman.

The Age of Elegance (1700-89)

The early years of the eighteenth century saw a continuation of the modes of the court of Louis XIV, and it was not until well into the first decade that the fashion muse took out her old farthingale, called it *paniers* or 'baskets', and put woman back inside an architectural structure. Three main shapes dominated the years from 1710 to 1780. Dome-shaped hoops of various dimensions were worn throughout the period, making the waist look disproportionately small, as may be seen in the example of 68-year-old Mrs Purefoy, a member of the English gentry, who wore a hoop that emphasized her waist of 'eighteen inches and a nail'; this is only one inch larger than the fictional 16-year-old Scarlett O'Hara in the 1850s, whose waist was the smallest in the three counties of the Southern States of America. During the years 1714 to 1730 the dome flattened into an oval shape, which developed into the wide oblong hoops worn in the middle of the century. In these structures the skirt hung over two vast side *paniers*, made from a basket-like material, and often stretched six feet from side to side, thus forcing ladies to walk sideways through doors, until collapsible *paniers* were invented to make the operation easier. Only the moneyed classes wore these vast oblong hoops, and they were *de rigueur* at the French and English courts. Over them was worn an open robe, fitted tightly to the bodiced figure and made of richly patterned embroidered silks and brocades and later of flowered chintz, with a V-shaped opening in the front revealing a decorative petticoat beneath. Quilted petticoats were worn for warmth, on informal occasions and as an alternative skirt support to the hoop. Bright colours, tiny bows and frills were favoured, giving an air of frivolity to any court function. Small neat hairstyles compensated for the extra width gained in the dress, these two factors together

Below: Signboard of the Art Dealer Gersain: *a painting by Antoine Watteau (1721), showing a lady in the saque garment, which later became known as the Watteau pleat. It was one of the few fashions to be initiated by an artist.*

27

Above: Thomas Gainsborough's portrait of Mary Countess Stowe (c. 1760) gives the light, airy feeling of the dress rather than paying minute attention to detail. The ruffled sleeves are typical of the period.

Right: A conversation piece showing an English family at tea in 1720, by Joseph Van Aken. The ladies are wearing typical two-piece gowns of the period. The seated woman on the left has her skirt gored to reveal a quilted petticoat.

making up the characteristic silhouette of the mid-eighteenth century. Mrs Delany, describing the English court in 1746 in her *Life and Letters*, writes: 'They curl and wear a great many *tawdry* things, but there is such a variety in the manner of dress, that I don't know what to tell you is the fashion; the only thing that seems general are hoops of enormous size, and most people wear vast *winkers* to their heads.' (Tawdry meant 'fanciful' at the time, and winkers were caps which spread out at the temples.)

France was the arbiter of fashion throughout the eighteenth century, Madame de Pompadour being one of her most glorious stars. Although she originated no new fashions, she set a standard of elegance in the delicacy and beauty of her clothes, their pretty bows and lace flouncing giving her an air of sumptuous lightness. The extravagant costume she perfected was to end only with the French Revolution.

salon, and Madame Geoffrin herself was so eminent a personality that when she stayed in Vienna the young Marie Antoinette came to meet her.

Marie Antoinette was possibly the most elegant lady of the century. Clothes were her passion and it is said that at her morning *levée* she had a palette containing swatches from all her dresses presented to her so that she could choose her outfit for the day. Her ladies-in-waiting were expected to take note and choose their *ensembles* accordingly. There were few dresses that Marie Antoinette wore more than twice; she had a positive mania for novelty and her caprices frequently led the ladies at Versailles to court financial ruin by their efforts to follow her example. One of her crazes, which must have infuriated the bourgeoisie, was her passion for dressing up in peasant costume and playing at shepherdesses at the Petit Trianon. This insensitivity combined with her blind

Elegance in a more simple style existed outside court circles, in the *salons* of the Paris intelligentsia. Hostesses like Madame Geoffrin, whose 'toilette can be summed up as the most careful simplicity combined with irreproachable neatness', were not dowdy blue-stockings but combined good conversation with *haute couture* and *haute cuisine*. Voltaire and Rousseau, Diderot and other Encyclopedists were frequent visitors to her

extravagance must certainly have helped to fan the flames of public disapproval that culminated in the French Revolution.

The Age of Enlightenment (1789-1836)

The chief aim of eighteenth-century women's dress had been to emphasize class distinctions, but no sooner did the French Revolution erupt with the storming of the Bastille in 1789 than this intention was reversed. It now became unfashionable to be fashionable and French women therefore strove to be as inconspicuous as possible. Hoops were gradually abandoned and a miscellany of peasant-type garments and scarves sporting the *tricolor* was adopted. Fashion lacked guidance for a brief few years until, during the Reign of Terror, a new line was created and a 'federal uniform' put many ladies into a simple enveloping garment with a sash as their only ornament. When the Directory was formed, in 1795, the mood changed yet again and the bourgeoisie, enjoying the social life of Paris for the first time, sought out clothing that would distinguish the fashionable partisan from her compatriots. Dresses became straight sheaths of thin muslin, sometimes tied by a coloured ribbon just below the bust. This costume was all-revealing, displaying the wearer's shape beneath the drapery. It was a style interpretation that harked back to ancient Greece and Rome, for in the aftermath of the Reign of Terror people were seeking a new meaning and order to their lives that the classical world could be said to symbolize. Women now adopted a stooping posture that was intended to represent an elegant Grecian bend, but as the moving figure found it

hard to imitate the classical line of a static piece of sculpture, the stance of Directory women was often the subject of satirical sketches.

New hairstyles added to the general effect of simplicity. The hair was short and now curled, in Greek fashion, close to the head, or was caught loosely at the back. One popular style, called 'à la sacrifice', brushed the hair forward over the top of the head as a playful reminder of the hair of a martyr of the guillotine, while a red ribbon 'à la victime' was worn round the neck as a macabre souvenir of the Reign of Terror.

The classical idiom remained in fashion throughout the years of Napoleon's influence, since an echo of the empires of antiquity suited his political ideals, but he felt that the near-nakedness of the Directory style did not become the new dignity of the state. Fashions therefore grew more sedate, and as a new aristocracy was gradually formed, costume was once again designed to display rank and wealth. Napoleon himself hated any suggestion of economy and expected women to dress lavishly, bringing the family pearls and diamonds out of hiding and rustling in yards of silk or satin. He allowed himself to rule as a dictator of fashion through his beautiful wife Josephine, whose taste was in the impeccable tradition of the elegant French

Above: The Hon. Mrs Graham, also painted by Thomas Gainsborough (c. 1765), is seen in an elaborate satin dress with a feather-trimmed hat perched on her high coiffure.

Left: Two costumes of 1791, showing how the French Revolution simplified dress, making plain peasant-style simplicity fashionable. The shape shows an exaggeration of the bust and the back is reinforced with a bustle. Fanciful head-dresses were sometimes worn as a celebration of the newly acquired liberty.

28. Cahier. 1791.

grande dame. He loved to see women in white, so his empress seldom dressed in any other colour, but even with such limitations she succeeded in dazzling both him and the whole court. At one ball shortly after she received her title in 1804 she was 'a vision in misty-white *mousseline de l'Inde,* with a narrow lamé border like a rivulet of gold round the hemline of the pleated skirt, a gold-and-black enamelled lion's head on each shoulder and another as a clasp on a gold belt'. (The costume is described by Laure Junot.) Napoleon was captivated and led her to a mirror so that he might see her from all sides at once. However the divorce that Josephine so much dreaded was near at hand. When the blow finally came in 1809 she retired to Malmaison with only her clothes to console her. Her obsession for dress continued and an inventory of her wardrobe at this time listed no less than 676 dresses, 49 court costumes, 252 hats and head-dresses, 60 cashmere shawls, 785 slippers, 413 pairs of stockings and 498 embroidered chemises.

Ladies at the English court could not boast of such vast wardrobes, for the mood of the time frowned on such excesses. Hoops were still worn for court occasions, whereas the rest of Europe

and the newly United States of America were already glorying in the freedom of the Empire fashions. For a brief period during the Napoleonic Wars, when the rest of the world was cut off from France, each country was forced to develop her own styles, but as soon as the wars ended France's dictatorship of fashion revived. In England this coincided with the Regency period, when fashionable belles were already shivering in flimsy white gowns in the sea breezes of Brighton or the health-giving air of Bath.

They did not have to freeze for much longer, for by the end of the 1820s clothing was becoming more voluminous. Skirts supported by petticoats flared into a trumpet shape at the hem, and bare arms were now encased in vast sleeves. Sleeves could use almost as much material as had a skirt in the previous decade and restricted movement above the elbow. This constriction reflected a change in woman's outlook: she was no longer a creature of fun and gaiety but a decorous being who spent her time in sedentary occupations. She heralded the Victorian age.

The Age of Decorum (1837-1900)

Many things conspired to make Queen Victoria's reign mark the opening of a

Above left: Mme de Pompadour, shown here in a portrait by Quentin de la Tour. She was fond of delicate little bows, lace at the elbows and tiny shoes, and made these the height of elegance in dress.

Above right: Marie Antoinette was known for her taste and elegance. This portrait of her was probably painted in the 1780s, by Lis-Louis Périn.

Opposite: Ladies wearing clothes that illustrate the 18th century taste for ornamentation. Aquatint by Louis de Carmontelle (1760).

Above: An 1830s afternoon gown showing the enlarged sleeves typical of the time. Fabrics with floral patterns enclosed within wide bands were popular also. The demure lady is from Achille Deveria's Quatre Heures du Soir.

new fashion era. She herself did not have a remarkable clothes sense, but her accession coincided with the end of the romantic fashions that succeeded the skimpy garments of the Empire. France was now ruled by the bourgeois king Louis-Philippe and his influence soon spread to England, where the atmosphere was ripe for a new type of figurehead. Queen Victoria, with her happy respectability, fulfilled this need, but she came in with the bourgeois fashion rather than introducing it.

The new emphasis on respectability was based on an appreciation of the value of work. Thus it was part of the nineteenth-century credo – not only in England but in Continental Europe and America too – that only the hard-working man could rise in the world. His industriousness was proved by the objects that exhibited the fruits of his efforts, such as his house, which grew more and more complex, thanks to the mistaken idea that layers of decoration over a plain surface are the best expression of wealth and status, and his wife now dressed, in keeping with the furniture, like a well-upholstered armchair (as William Morris despairingly noted). Her skirts grew wider and wider to demonstrate not only her right to a place in the world but also the fact that her husband could afford the vast yardage required by such dimensions.

In his capacity as an industrialist the husband was also helping to develop new fabrics, thus bringing them within the range of income groups who had not been able to afford many new clothes in the previous century. Fashion was beginning to spread its nets far wider. As the *English Gentlewoman* noted in 1845, 'Young ladies, from the middling classes upwards, wear very much the same materials of dress, frequent the same dressmakers, and adopt the same style of hair as those which are in vogue amongst the highest classes.' The highest classes could not even distinguish themselves from the lower orders in their choice of colours, for purple – that rare colour once worn only by kings and emperors – was suddenly displayed everywhere when a British chemist, W.H. (later Sir William) Perkin discovered in 1856 a way of making violet dye cheaply from coal-tar products. These aniline dyes, as they were known, were extremely popular, though the colours were bright and crude and even dangerous. The colour green was quickly abandoned when it was found to contain a poisonous substance, though not before one belle had been killed by her green ball dress!

Other innovations brought fashions nearer to the ordinary girl who was trying to look pretty on a small budget. Fashion magazines in England started to carry paper patterns regularly in 1860 when Mrs Beeton included them in *The Englishwoman's Domestic Magazine* and Butterick's in America began printing patterns in 1863. Magazines also carried instructions on making up and

Right: This satirical engraving of the 1860s illustrates the problems of the crinoline skirt. The tiny parasol mocks the fashion for carrying parasols as decorative accessories rather than for protective purposes.

on converting last year's garments to suit this year's fashions, thus tacitly acknowledging the needs of the girl who could not afford to leave everything to her dressmaker. The sewing machine was also coming into general use. One version seems to have been made in about 1829 by a French tailor named Barthélemy Thimonnier, but Elias Howe in the United States patented the first effective sewing machine in 1845. He did not, however, have the business sense and marketing genius of his compatriot, Isaac Singer, who patented a machine in 1851 and immediately opened up a chain of shops in England and the United States.

With this invention came the beginning of the ready-to-wear trade in clothes. Until this time women buying a 'gown' had in fact bought a dress-length complete with trimmings, which they then had made up by their own dressmaker. This situation infuriated the busy Jane Austen, who wrote to her sister Cassandra in 1798, 'I cannot determine what to do about my new gown! I wish such things were to be bought ready made.' By the mid-nineteenth century this desire had been fulfilled and women were able to buy ready-made or partly-made garments over the counter.

It was also possible now to buy much more cheaply the substructures on which the fashion shape rested. The cage crinoline, invented in 1856, brought wide skirts to all ladies, maid-servants and factory hands. (There is an ironic twist in this, since the original intention of the crinoline skirt had been to widen class differences by creating a physical distance between the social strata.) Yet parallel to the new inventions designed to level out class distinctions in dress ran the desire of every *nouvelle riche* to demonstrate her altered status. This perhaps explains why fashions changed so rapidly in the nineteenth century, for if one's maid could afford to copy one's styles, constant novelty was the only way to keep her at bay, at least for a year or two.

But though fashions varied, there were a few mainline shapes. The crinoline skirt reached its greatest size in the 1860s but by 1870 had declined. It was replaced by the bustle, which supported the skirt at the back and held it up in a large puff to reveal a decorative petticoat beneath. The bustle style produced an elegant shape at first but, like the crinoline, suffered from exaggeration. By 1888 it was jutting out like a shelf 'whereon a good-sized tea-tray might be carried'. At this time trimmings, too, were at their most absurd. One could have collected from dresses and hats whole collections of stuffed or imitation birds, beetles, butterflies, centipedes, lizards, mice, monkeys, rats, snakes, spiders and flies. Long trains were worn in the evenings, requiring many yards of trimmings and often sewn with metal or jet beads, sequins and imitation pearls. This over-decoration possibly

Above: By 1873, when Ernest Duez painted this afternoon walk, the bustle was back in favour. Here the skirt is held back by a large black bow, and the pretty frills on the underskirt are displayed to view.

Left: Two ladies in more softly flowing crinolines, lithograph by Boutet de Monuel, c. 1860.

Jeune Francaise allant au Champ de Mars faire l'Exercice

Opposite: Detail from
Jacques-Louis David's The
Consecration of the Emperor
Napoleon I and the Corona-
tion of the Empress
Josephine (1804). Her
gown shows a nostalgia for
mediaeval dress.

Above: Thomas Lawrence's
portrait of Queen Charlotte
(1789) illustrates the
formality of the English court
which contrasted sharply with
the freer clothes of revolutionary France.

Above right: A revolutionary
partisan sports the tricolor
and military type clothing, as
she sets off for training in the
Champ de Mars in Paris
(1789).

Right: An 18th century
caricaturist mocks the
costume of the belles of
Brighton in 1810. Their thin
clothing scarcely covers the
breasts, and clings to every
curve.

Above: In 1885 the bustle created a shelf-like effect at the back, as this day-dress shows. The looped draperies are reminiscent of the 'polonaise' style of the 18th century.

Above right: Princess Victoria of Prussia, Queen Victoria's favourite daughter, photographed in a neat tailored walking suit in 1886. The picture illustrates the hour glass silhouette which was popular at this time. It was achieved by tight corsetting at the waist and padding on bust and hips.

compensated for the low-cut *décolletage*, which was clearly not in keeping with the prudery of the mid-Victorian age. Even so, costumes at the close of the century were excessively tight, skirts were long and hampering and women's clothes, with the exception of sports clothes (see Chapter 4), showed few signs of emancipation, though their wearers were firmly proving their worth in professional fields.

A Breath of Air (1900-1970s)

At the beginning of the twentieth century women in Britain and the United States were fighting for the vote, but their clothes were still constricting. The figure assumed an elegant S-curve with the bosom pushed forwards and the hips backwards. Pretty lace blouses with feminine flouncing emphasized the forward thrust of the body and a large hat and parasol completed the silhouette. It was an attractive shape, but it distorted the body's natural proportions and kept women firmly in their place as decorative objects. Even the increasing

popularity of sport and new activities such as motoring did little to make women's clothes more convenient, though it is astonishing how active women managed to be in the first decade of the century.

Fashions were gradually moving towards greater freedom when the First World War broke out in 1914 and temporarily curtailed the activities of fashion designers. When the war was over women rebelled against the state of subjection in which they had been held for so long. They had proved their capacity for work during the war and now sought acceptance as the equals of men. They emphasized this by adopting masculine attitudes, cutting their hair short like a boy's and compressing their figures into a tube shape that denied all trace of femininity. A straight shift was worn with a belt over the hips and a cloche hat concealed the hair. Arms were bare, and more of the legs was revealed as the twenties advanced. (In 1928–9 skirts even became longer at the back than at the front.) It was a simple and

economical style requiring little skill in creation and few or no foundation garments. It therefore appealed to an even wider range of women than the inventions of the industrial age had been able to attract and was well suited to a period of financial depression. One shift could serve many occasions, since it could be embellished in a variety of ways, perhaps with long strings of beads hanging down to the hem, or with ribbons or a scarf tied to the belt.

During the thirties, though the world economy was still in a state of flux, women's fashions became more complex and more difficult for the working girl to copy. The line of the dress was more feminine and alluring, cleverly cut so that the garment hugged the figure closely to reveal the natural contours and then flowed out in a long skirt, a line typified by Vionnet's clothes. A less complicated silhouette had been popularized by Coco Chanel, the most influential designer of the twenties, who introduced inconspicuous elegance in her timeless easy skirt and jersey jacket

(which have changed little today).

There was a marked distinction between day clothes and evening wear, so that the factory girl who wore cotton dungarees during the day would reserve a smart suit or a shiny black satin cocktail dress for special occasions. The lower classes were meanwhile drawing so near to their 'betters' that it soon needed an expert to distinguish between an *haute couture* model and its popular copy. Two factors were responsible for this state of affairs: the increasing efficiency and speed of mass production; and the development of technology, in particular the successful production of man-made fibres.

In spite of this, however, it was a shortage of materials that prompted the British Board of Trade in 1941 to design an economical garment when the Second World War had once again shaken up the fashion world. This 'Utility clothing' as it was called, threw the emphasis on economy of cut and hard-wearing qualities. Suitable garments were guaranteed with the government stamp CC41. This was a time of rationing in Britain, so women had to be very careful how they spent their annual supply of 40 coupons: one suit used up 18 coupons and a dress twelve. In the affluent United States government regulations also kept a check on the amount of material that manufacturers were allowed to use in

Left: In 1901 the S-curve is already pronounced in this afternoon dress by Paquin. This was achieved by the use of a corset which drove the stomach slanting inwards so that the bust overhung the waist. Femininity is reinforced by the broderie anglaise, and Renaissance-style sleeves.

Below: Less romantically dressed are these girls in a Manchester shirt factory in 1909, though they too wear soft, lacy blouses. The centre parting and pulled back hair gives them a severe appearance.

Left: A riding-dress of c. 1835, showing the accentuated sleeves typical of the time; painting by Achille Deveria: Sept Heures du Matin. *Ladies' sporting clothes borrowed features from men's dress.*

Above: Richard Redgrave: The Governess (1844). *The girls are wearing typically Victorian frocks; the governess being kept firmly in her place by the uniform of black dress and white collar.*

Right: Detail from Franz Xavier Winterhalter's portrait of the Princesse de Joinville. The hairstyle and dropped shoulder line is typical of the 1840s and 1850s.

Right: A dress by the Spanish- born designer Fortuny, c. 1912, made in apricot pleated silk.

Far right: A black dress from Dior's first collection in 1947, showing the features of the New Look, full calf length skirt, plunge neckline, three-quarter length batwing sleeves.

Below: Two 'bright young things' in dresses of 1928. The girl on the left wears a straight chemise with dropped waistline and wide brimmed cloche hat. The girl on the right wears a dress with uneven hemline, dipping at the back, a fashion which attempted a compromise between short and long skirts.

Below right: In the thirties long skirts and more feminine lines were back in fashion. This drawing from a mail order catalogue shows frocks for a hostess and her dinner guests in 1934, a year in which puffed sleeves were high fashion.

The uneven hem-line dipping at the back is expressed to perfection in this beautiful dress of tiered lace, which is one of many lovely models at Selfridges, Oxford Street, W.

Left: A tailor-made skirt of 1937, seen here with a typical French accessory – the beret.

Below: Women workers in King's Road, Chelsea, London, during the Second World War wearing boiler suits for convenience. Such garments had a lasting influence on the woman's image.

one garment, and Mainbocher designed an economical – but chic – uniform for the women's forces.

This shortage of materials made the success of Dior's New Look, launched in Paris in 1947, all the more remarkable. Not only was it his first collection, but it required a great deal of material for its wide full skirt. It was popular because it was a move towards femininity, with natural rounded shoulders replacing the square military cut. Dior remained the most influential designer until 1957 when Balenciaga brought in the chemise or sack dress. Dior himself had forecast the general mood of a return to the shapes of the twenties with his H-line and A-line of 1954 and 1955. He had also revived interest in a shortened form of the 'crinoline' skirt, though this was not to be fully realized until the teenage fashions of the late fifties seized upon paper nylon petticoats that were being produced cheaply. Young girls could now wear pretty waisted frocks with wide knee-length skirts and rustling petticoats.

Since then fashions have fluctuated from year to year, changing faster in a season than during twenty years in the eighteenth century. This is partly because fashionable clothes are now

41

Opposite: White evening dress emphasizing a pinched-in waist and low décolletage. Une Soirée, painting by Jean Béraud (1878).

Below: Cover from the French magazine, Art, Gout, Beauté (1929). By this date skirts were down to below the knee. The picture also shows the bias cut, which was to alter the silhouette of the thirties.

Below: Tailored suits in a fashion plate of c. 1900 forming the typically Edwardian 's' curve. The exaggerated hats elongate the figure.

Bottom: A bronze figure of a girl symbolizing the dancing twenties. She is dressed in the typical skirt and sweater of 1925 with the obligatory cloche hat.

CROISETTE. — Crêpe   Chemisier A. G. B.

Création ♥ Premet

Façon Tailleur

Above: A loose-weave tweed coat showing the chic line of the early sixties, from Balmain's collection in 1963. The style is basically a continuation of themes of the fifties, full skirts, wide coats, small hats and always matching accessories.

Above right: Dior's A line was launched in 1955. This picture shows a classical checked tweed suit with pleated skirt to give the A-shape flare.

cheaper, with the result that constant novelty can be both sought and supplied; and partly because in an age when all women work (or have worked) the need for convenient yet varied clothing has finally been recognized. The main trends in the last decade are discussed in the postscript. Basically fashion designers offered women two shapes – the leggy look of the miniskirt and hot pants and the classical line achieved by the maxi and midi.

If one regards the slow revolution towards democratic clothing that breaks down class barriers as starting in the age of the Enlightenment, at the time of the French Revolution, one is struck by the fact that it has taken almost two hundred years for the ideal to be achieved. Today we regard simple, cheap and attractive clothing as the birthright of all social classes, but we forget how our prede-

cessors suffered either from a conscious-
ness of their own inferiority of position,
or at the other end of the scale from the
discomfort of constricting finery. Today's women are fortunate, too, in that
their shapes are at last their own and
each individual may choose a costume
that enhances her best features.

*Right: A typical woman's
shape of 1969 – leggy,
carefree and all-revealing.
Dress by Ricki Reed, with
tights by Mary Quant.*

*Left: Two midi dresses
designed for the house of
Dior in 1970, illustrating a
re-echo of the A-line. The two
coats are trimmed with black
snake-skin creating patterns
which show the influence of
graphics on fashion.*

Chapter Three

Conscious Display

Class Distinction

'Dress is a very foolish thing,' Lord Chesterfield says, 'and yet it is a very foolish thing for a man not to be well dressed according to his rank and way of life.' It was foolish because a man, or woman, of 'quality' had to retain his position by frank displays of wealth and class, particularly by piling on unnecessary or costly accessories. During the Renaissance both men and women achieved this by the use of elaborate hats and head-dresses, ruffs and gem-encrusted embroideries. In the eighteenth and nineteenth centuries it was equally easy to show off one's leisured status by wearing elaborate clothing, which proved that a valet or maid was in attendance, or inconvenient garments which, by restricting movement, indicated that the wearer was not compelled to do physical labour. For men there was the hidden encumbrance of corset stays, which pulled in his waist to the point where even bending to pick up a dropped handkerchief was a strain. Similarly their tight pantaloons required considerable ingenuity and effort to get into, so much so that George Washington, when a young dandy of eighteen, is said to have hung his up on pegs and then jumped into them to ensure a snug fit.

Women too were stiffened by their corsets, petticoat and fashion substructures and by outward signs such as choker collars that made them look as if they were being elegantly strangled. Other encumbrances were high hairstyles that required a scrupulously erect carriage; tiny embroidered shoes designed for walking no further than to the next chair; handkerchiefs too small for use; fans that looked pretty but were too small to refresh; sleeves so tight that any movement was restricted; and unnecessary overgarments and trimmings whose sole purpose was to demonstrate that the wearer could afford to indulge in them. Yet the lady of leisure wore these clothes with an air of nonchalant arrogance for, as a book on etiquette of 1836 cautioned: 'Be not conspicuously careful about the safety of your dress in company, lest it be supposed you carry your wardrobe on your back.'

The desire to impress 'company' was no doubt one of the reasons underlying the absurd social calls of the period, which lasted just long enough for each party to display himself or herself to his host and then depart, before conversation necessitated any more intimate contact. Yet for the more fashionable ladies of the third quarter of the eighteenth century this duty must have involved considerable discomfort, for some would have been forced to kneel down on the floor of their sedan chairs to make way for their towering head-dresses.

The Hair

The shape of the head and hairstyle has always been one of the most prominent features of the silhouette. At the beginning of the eighteenth century men wore more elaborate hairstyles than women,

Opposite: Pre-Raphaelite clothing harks back to the opulence of the Renaissance in the voluminous sleeves and accessories as in this portrait of Mona Vanna in 1886 by Dante Gabriel Rossetti.

Below: A French outfit of the 1770s exhibits details intended to stress class distinction. Only high-born ladies could afford to wear movement-constricting side-paniers and high hairstyles which took hours to construct. The roses, ribbons and ruchings which decorate the dress show that costly labour has been expended on the lady's finery. Engraving by Voisard.

Above: Dr Johnson wearing a wig and frock coat, painted by Sir Joshua Reynolds, 1756.

Below: William Hogarth's The Five Orders of Perriwigs *(1761), satirizes the excess of gentlemen's wigs in the eighteenth century.*

Below right: Four drawings of 1776, show how a lady's looks may be 'improved' by fanciful head-dresses, each design being given a romantic or seductive name.

since most women adopted a cap that effectively covered the hair, while men were decked in a variety of wigs. The most popular were the full-bottomed wig with a mass of curls framing the face, favoured by the elderly and the learned professions; the bob wig, which had a long or a short bob tied at the back with a ribbon bow; the bag wig, which had a long queue enclosed in a square silk bag; the pig-tail wig, which was spirally bound and sometimes stiffened to bend up at the back; and the Ramillies wig, a long plait tied with ribbons at top and bottom. Wigs were generally powdered grey, white being used only for full-dress occasions.

A gentleman would have a contract with a wigmaker to keep him in fashion and to keep his head cut close or even shaved, as he was bald beneath his wig. Henry Purefoy, a squire of Shalstone in Berkshire and son of the tiny-waisted Mrs Purefoy, wrote a number of letters that reveal the sartorial concerns of men of his class. In 1747, for instance, he wrote to his wigmaker: 'The new periwigg you made me has some Hair on the top of the Crown that don't curl and when I put on my hat or the wind blows it stares and rises all up. I have minded other folks' periwiggs and I think I should have another row of curls higher towards ye Crown. Pray don't make my other wigs so, for you must alter this that I have.'

More exotic wigs were constantly being tried, but perhaps none is more amazing than the one worn by Lady Mary Wortley Montagu's mad son Edward. Horace Walpole describes him: 'He diamonds himself even to distinct shoe buckles for a frock; and has more snuff boxes than would suffice a Chinese idol with a hundred noses. But the most curious part of his dress, which he has brought back from Paris, is an Iron wig; you literally would not know it from hair.'

Women did wear wigs but to nothing like the same extent that men did and indeed some did have false hair threaded into their own. Feminine hairstyles reached their height in the 1770s, and they were certainly very high. The Empress Maria Theresa wrote to her daughter, Marie Antoinette, in 1775: '...They say that your coiffure rises 36 inches... and is decorated with a mass of feathers and ribbons which make it

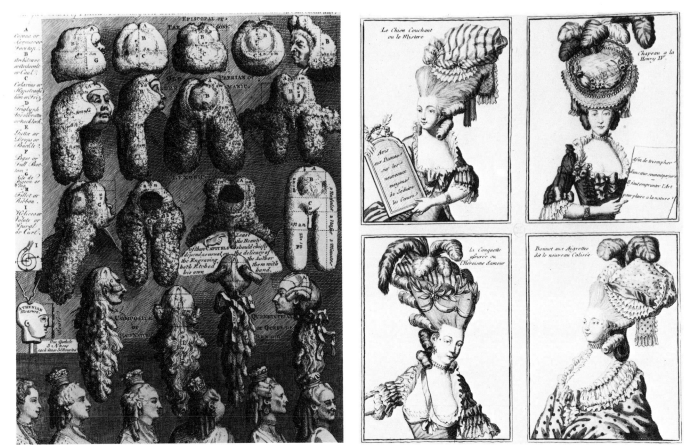

even higher.... I was always of the opinion that one should follow the fashions with restraint but never exaggerate them.' That women in fact had very little restraint is shown by the abundance of satirical drawings of this period. Hairstyles were loaded with flowers, bird of paradise, a kitchen garden, a plate of fruit or even a ship in full sail. These structures were so elaborate that once dressed, a lady's coiffure was expected to last at least a month, and often two months, no doubt with unsavoury results, since the hair would be mingled with lard and whiting to keep it in place. The nocturnal mouse was a continual hazard. It must have been uncomfortable enough to sleep with one's head propped carefully on cushions, but the weight of a mouse-resistant nightcap must have come near to preventing sleep altogether. The *London Magazine* (with tongue in cheek) speaks of a silversmith in London's New Bond Street in 1779 who had invented 'nightcaps so strong that no mouse or even a rat can gnaw through them. The present demand for these articles is incredible. They are sold at 3 gns each but the *ton* have them of gilt wire from 6–10 guineas.' Perhaps at no other period was the difference between rich and poor expressed so graphically as in these high head-dresses.

By the 1790s false hair was only occasionally worn in Britain, and the hair-powder tax imposed by the government in 1795 effectively put a stop to this fashion. Never again was so much fanciful attention lavished on the hair, but styles did continue to develop along more modest lines. A women would train her tresses to grow in short curls or long ringlets to prove that no trimmings were needed to detract from the natural softness of her crowning glory. Her only aids were invisible pads and nets to keep the hair in the required shape. Victorian fashions favoured long hair – religiously brushed a hundred times a day – tied back tightly over the ears and contained in a chignon at the nape of the neck or allowed to curl in tight ringlets that were painstakingly pressed into shape by a curling iron heated in the fire. A variety of hairstyles was evolved to suit the rapid changes in the silhouette during the nineteenth century and most of them required the help of a maid or sister. It was not until the 1870s, in the wake of the Rational Dress Campaign, that a freer style emerged in the United States, from where it soon spread to Europe. The hair was allowed to hang loosely at the back, caught only by a clasp or ribbon.

Apart from a brief vogue at the time of the Empire, short hair for women made its first appearance after the First World War when, in keeping with their boyish dress, girls wore their hair

Left: The arts involved in hairdressing led this satirist to design an American version, entitled Bunker's Hill, 1776.

Below: Victorian women were expected to brush out their long hair a hundred times a day and it was considered a great virtue to be able to sit on it. However hardly anyone saw their hair in all its glory, as it was nearly always coiled into a neat bun at the back of the head. Women in rational dress in the 1850s are seen here taking a morning's walk hatless – an innovation of the campaign.

cropped, bobbed or shingled. It was woman's most drastic action of rebellion against the state of subjection in which she had been held for centuries. In the thirties hair was allowed to grow once again and for some years was worn in short, close to the head, but softer styles. One that disguised the length of the hair involved brushing it into a crown of short curls on top of the head. (This was the style chosen for copying by the nostalgic girl of the early seventies who looked back to the sophistication of an earlier age.) This was not, however, the most typical style of the decade, as it suited few women. Most wore their hair to just below ear-level, with a side or centre parting and waves carefully 'ironed' into place with hair tongs. During the forties and fifties Hollywood filmstars set the trend towards ringlets and curls, until the vogue came in for a windswept look that gave the straight-haired girls a chance to appear to

Opposite: Le Comte de Vaudreuil *by Germain Drouais, 1758.*

Above left: A satirical drawing entitled The Triumph of Liberty, *c. 1789.*

Above right: The Progress of the Toilet *by James Gillray,*

Below: Hairstyles by Vidal Sassoon, 1972–3.

advantage for the first time for some generations. This developed in the sixties into the page-boy cut, which framed the face with a demure fringe (bangs) and had hair curling under at the shoulders – a re-echo of Renaissance boys' fashions. Meanwhile men tried to assert their lost right to long hair in neo-cavalier styles, though shoulder-length hair has not been associated with high fashion for men in the seventies.

Modern hairstyling with its sophisticated techniques of tinting, dyeing, straightening and permanent waving has been responsible for innumerable changes of style since the Second World

buy it as not. I shall pull it to pieces as soon as I get home, and see if I can make it up any better.' Hours were spent in millinery shops looking for ribbons, flowers, fruit and feathers to adorn a new hat. Sometimes the trimmings reached monstrous proportions, serving as a kind of advertising poster to draw attention to the diminutive figure beneath. At other times, usually when the hairstyle was an important feature, the hat was no more than a small cap perched on top of the head.

Some kind of head covering was worn by women of all classes both indoors and out. The cap worn indoors changed very

Above: Women's hats were enormous in the 1830s, not quite as big as this, but the cartoonist's pen was always ready to point out absurdities in the fashions. Most hats were high-crowned, wide brimmed and elaborately trimmed with huge bows and feathers.

Right: Trying on bonnets at a milliner's in 1828. Hats were slowly growing larger.

Below: Princess Margaret wearing a scarf, jumper and skirt and Antony Armstrong-Jones equally democratically clad in a fisherman's smock and boots in 1965.

War; indeed the economics of hair-dressing make it imperative for the stylist to bring in new lines that a woman could not create for herself. Although hair accessories are rarely used, the well-dressed head is still a masterpiece of creative skill that draws the observer's attention.

Hats, Ribbons and Scarves

Hats and bonnets changed from year to year to match the minor fluctuations of dress styles, and much of a woman's time was spent in making or remaking a bonnet. Many, like Lydia Bennet in Jane Austen's *Pride and Prejudice,* seem to have enjoyed the activity for its own sake. 'Look here,' she says, 'I have bought this bonnet. I do not think it is very pretty; but I thought I might as well

little during the eighteenth and nineteenth centuries. Basically it was designed to protect the hair, but frills or lappets also framed the face attractively. A night mob was worn even in bed, since it was considered indecent for any woman, except a very young girl, to appear with her head uncovered even before her husband and servants and it also provided a little extra warmth.

The last flowering of the hat, before the ubiquitous cloche of the twenties submerged all individuality, came in the Edwardian age, when it was at its most charming and least ridiculous. The large straw sun hat decorated with ribbons has survived until the 1970s, but only for occasions such as big weddings or race meetings or grand garden parties. The cloche hat was a decided class

Since the eighteenth century jewelry has been an ideal vehicle for gratuitously displaying riches, since it had no obvious use. For men it took the form of expensive watch-chains, diamond-studded shoe buckles, scent bottles, snuff boxes, and useless toys and trinkets which reached their peak of extravagance in Fabergé's confections of the 1870s and 1880s. Even buttons were used to add to the conspicuous taste for luxury that over-embellished everything. Two or three buttons were all that was required to fasten a coat at the waist, and in the 1770s and 1780s the rest could be worn to present a walking picture gallery, exquisitely painted or inlaid to show a favourite belle, a bunch of flowers, a pretty shepherdess or more *risqué* subjects with titles such as 'The Loves of Aretino', painted in the manner of Watteau, Greuze, Boucher and Vanloo. More ostentatious were the jewelled buttons of the type worn by the Comte d'Artois, who had a set of diamond buttons, each of which encased a miniature watch. The French Revolution brought more simple metal buttons for all classes and patriots wore them decorated with trees of liberty or the *tricolor*.

American buttons, reflecting the Puritans' taste for sobriety, were examples of simple, honest craftsmanship. Many were made of plain solid silver or pewter, though the more common materials were pearl and bone. The Americans too had their commemorative buttons, many different types being made for delegates to George Washington's inauguration ceremony. These were stamped with such devices as an eagle with a sun or star above its head, or a shining sun with the legend 'The Majesty of the People'.

It was Beau Brummell in the early nineteenth century who was responsible for introducing a note of sobriety into men's costume; he decreed – and in the world of fashion his word was law – that a diamond solitaire cravat pin and a modest signet ring were all that a fashionable man should wear. There were, however, no restrictions on the wearing of jewels by women. By 1725 Brazilian and Indian diamonds had

leveller; it was simple enough to be within the means of any working girl, the only specification being that she should wear her hair as short as the boyish fashions demanded. Fancy shawls were sometimes worn in the twenties in place of a hat, either draped over the shoulders or wrapped seductively round both head and shoulders. Scarves were worn tied to the waist-belt in long loops to vary the rigid lines of the chemise skirt.

In the 1940s scarves descended to the level of a thing of utility, becoming the popular triangular headscarf for protecting the hair in bad weather. This was popularized in Britain by Princess Elizabeth and Princess Margaret, and is still worn at all levels of society in both Europe and the United States, illustrating the modern trend towards sartorial equality. Hats on the whole have now been abandoned, except for formal social occasions. Caps and berets still enjoy popularity for winter warmth and the vogue for long skirts and dresses in the seventies has sometimes been accompanied by elaborate or fanciful hats for day wear.

Jewelry

In the course of the last 250 years fashionable jewelry has undergone a transformation from fabulously expensive items of luxury display to cheap plastic beads and cut-glass stones available to every person who feels a desire for that glitter which, according to

Left: An evening shawl of 1929 which shows the influence of the Bauhaus movement in art. Scarves and shawls were frequently worn in the twenties to relieve the plainness of outline of the chemise dress.

Below: A gentleman in 1777 dazzles his lady friend with his cut-steel buttons. His shoes have Artois buckles and his hat is a tricorne. She wears a pyramid hairstyle and a bouquet in her bosom.

Above: Jacques-Louis David's portrait of his doctor, Alphonse Leroy, wearing a turban and banyan, or Indian nightgown, which was worn by gentlemen of the 18th and early 19th centuries on informal occasions.

become quite common and most members of the European aristocracy owned a *parure* of diamond necklace and matching earrings. Bracelets were popular and often had watches set into them, encrusted with diamonds. Pearls, too, have been popular at various times. In the eighteenth century, for instance, there was a taste for wearing a single drop pearl fastened to a narrow ribbon round the neck, while in the early twentieth century strings of single, double or triple pearls were the hallmark of the chic woman.

Imitation jewelry began to be produced in Paris in about 1730, but it was Matthew Boulton of Birmingham who really popularized what became known

as 'costume' jewelry when he evolved cut steel and marcasite jewelry designs. Throughout the nineteenth century women wore brightly coloured glass stones glistening in pinchbeck mounts. The society woman of course looked down on these imitations and wore only the rare stones herself. It was not until Chanel launched a fashion for crystal or coloured glass jewelry in the 1920s – a fashion that in the 1970s has still not died out – that costume jewelry became not only fashionable but acceptable to the rich. The individualist, however, prefers not to decorate herself with necklaces or rings that have been stamped out by the thousand. Ornaments still have a rarity value even when

Left: J.A.J. Aved's portrait of Madame Crozat, Marquise du Châtel (1730–50), shows the mob cap worn at home.

Below: Watteau de Lille's picture of ladies in a French park shows the popular large hats and bonnets used to cover ornate hairstyles (1778).

Above: The First Earring, *engraved by William Chevalier after David Wilkie (1838), showing a young girl having her ears pierced. She already has a bracelet and is dressed as a miniature version of her mother.*

Opposite: A lady with a parasol from Sunday Afternoon on the Island of of la Grande Jatte *by Georges Seurat (late 19th century), showing the popular silhouette of the time. The women's hats are very similar to the man's.*

the materials themselves are not expensive. The Art Nouveau movement in the 1890s broke the tyranny of the precious stone by showing that it was possible to make beautiful jewelry using precious metals and enamel. With the revival of this movement in the sixties and seventies, jewelry again became the medium for really creative imagination after a long period of comparatively unexciting conventionality. The younger generation took to wearing chunky silver jewelry – heavy pendants adorned with large pebbles, rings on every finger or long drop earrings. Inspiration came from nature: from flower forms and crystalline structures. New materials such as perspex were used to create original ornaments and brought attractive jewelry – without a jewel – within the range of all. The modern trend in expensive jewelry is towards an exploration of the different textures that can be achieved with precious metals

and gems – in marked contrast to the symmetry of design demanded by previous generations.

Canes and Umbrellas

The cane or walking stick that was carried by gentlemen when swords were no longer necessary was an addition to masculine plumage and another mark of class distinction. After all, what working-class man could afford an ivory cane on which 93 rubies were spirally mounted, with a pair of field glasses cunningly tucked inside? Only someone of the standing of the Prussian Emperor Ferdinand III could feel himself entitled to such an object. Most gentlemen had dozens of canes, one to suit every mood or occasion, and perhaps to give them a sense of their own power. Voltaire, though no beau, had 80 canes, and even Rousseau, who prided himself on his sartorial simplicity, owned forty.

Women also carried canes, some of which had toilet mirrors, perfume bottles or amorous pictures concealed in the handle. Others had entertainment value, since they might have a musical box or even a pochette violin tucked inside the top.

As for the umbrella, that hallmark of the true-bred Englishman, it did not begin to be modish until 1800. Its success was in part due to the patronage of the Duke of Wellington, though he himself was startled at a uniquely British incident when at Bayonne he saw his officers, in the throes of battle, protecting their uniforms from the rain with umbrellas. The Duke sent a message saying he did 'not approve of the use of umbrellas during the enemy's firing and will not allow gentlemen's sons to make themselves ridiculous in the eyes of the army'.

Yet the common men of the army, whatever they thought during the campaign, were not slow to copy their superiors, who, anxious to retain the upper hand, instituted a series of fashions for the correct use of the umbrella, which in its early form was a clumsy object in any circumstances. For instance, it was vulgar to hold it under your arm like a walking stick, and the aristocracy held it by the middle, with the handle turned towards the ground. Only blue and green silk were *de bon ton.*

When it was found that the lower orders were quickly following suit, 'upper-class' umbrellas grew slimmer. Above all, the umbrella was a more or less useless accessory. It was certainly not intended to beat the rain, since it always had to appear neatly furled. If it looked like rain the fashionable man of the late nineteenth century simply hailed a cab. The unfashionable Londoner, however, could hire an umbrella from one of a series of umbrella stations for an average of four pence for three hours.

Umbrellas for ladies were a novelty in the early eighteenth century, but they never became a common accessory and women who carried them ran the risk of arousing their neighbours' derision. A Connecticut belle had one that had been sent to her from the West Indies in 1794, but her neighbours mocked her by carrying sieves balanced on broom handles whenever she passed. By the end of the century umbrellas were being sold in all milliners' shops, though it was not until the Victorian age that they became a common sight. They were still extremely clumsy and untidy objects and when worn in conjunction with the 'ugly' or poke bonnet presented a formidable appearance. For elegance rather than practicability, nothing surpassed the dainty parasol, which ladies carried about with the express purpose of appearing charming. It is true that it also acted as a sunshade, but it was essen-

tially a decorative object. As a fashion writer in *The Lewes & Brighthelmstone Journal* confessed in 1823, 'It is the fashion now not to hold up the parasol for it only prevents the men getting a glimpse at us, but merely carry it dangling in the hand to shew that you've got one.'

The parasol added to a lady's physical presence in the same way as a large hat or wide skirt, making her indisputably more noticeable. Most parasols were made of plain silk covered with black or white lace, and had elegantly carved handles of ivory, perhaps inlaid with coral or mother-of-pearl. From the mid-nineteenth century onwards, a hinge at the top of the parasol made the dome tilt backwards, so that the angle could be varied according to the sun. It complemented the backward thrust of the dress and gave a curving silhouette, as in Seurat's painting *La Grande Jatte*. In Edwardian times, when the parasol was at its most charming, the S-curve of the figure was greatly enhanced by the tilt of the sunshade. But the parasol, being essentially an encumbrance, vanished for ever with the days of freer activity stimulated by the two world wars.

The Useless Accessory

Most of the accessories mentioned in this chapter were worn, carried or kept with the intention of preserving a distance between the owner and the class of person to which he or she felt superior. The more useless it was the more it displayed conscious wealth. One of the most ridiculous of such displays was the retinue that accompanied a fashionable couple on their Sunday walk – an occasion when they were dressed to be seen by others. The Southern belle in America thought she cut a much finer figure if her Negro house servants followed her, dressed in descending degrees of finery according to their position, while the English lady liked to be seen with an Indian footman, gorgeously attired, walking ahead of her and a servant leading an ornamental dog following behind.

The cult of being seen with ornamental animals persisted throughout the eighteenth and nineteenth centuries. Lap dogs were the perfect accessories of indolence, since they required no

Above: Thomas Gainsborough's portrait of his doctor, Rice Charleton (1764) in a black frock coat. The doctor carries a silver topped cane, and wears a tricorne hat.

Below: A City gentleman in London in 1968 with typical men's accessories – neatly furled umbrella, bowler hat with a curly brim, fob watch, silk tie and breast pocket handkerchief.

Opposite: Fragonard's famous painting of 'The Swing' reveals the frilly undergarments of the 18th century, which were designed to attract attention on occasions such as these.

Below: Victorian outdoor garments feature long shawls and small hats; painting by Giulio Carmignani (mid-19th century).

Opposite below: A lady with a lap dog and a most unusual hat. La belle strasbourgeoise by Nicholas Largillière (probably 1740–50). She wears a single band of pearls round her neck and a fine lace fichu tucked into her corsage.

exercise. Thus Lady Bertram in Jane Austen's *Mansfield Park* 'spent her days sitting, nicely dressed on a sofa, doing some long piece of needlework of little use and no beauty, thinking more of her pug than her children...'. It was a fashion that can have had little attraction for men. After a bill for women's votes had been defeated in 1870, *Punch* asked what else one could expect, for:

Would you then know my Celia's charms?
She carries pug-dogs in her arms;
E'er dresses in the newest taste,
By lacing tight deforms her waist,
Bears on her head a brigand's hat,
Gay feathers flaunting high on that,
Her hair is only half her own,
The other half elsewhere has grown;
Her cheeks a dab of rouge reveal,
Her boots three inches high of heel.

Could such a creature as this be taken seriously?

Towards the end of Edward VII's reign *Punch* declared: 'The cult of the toy dog has reached a stage when ladies have to look at the little darlings through a microscope.' The 'little darlings' were tiny pomeranians, miniature pug dogs, decked out in ribbons matching those of their mistresses. Parrots, canaries, goldfish and monkeys also had their vogue as accessories to woman's vanity. They were replaced in the mid-twentieth century by the poodle – a familiar companion for the Hollywood filmstar in the forties – on whom dog-owners lavished an extraordinary amount of sartorial attention.

Undergarments

So far we have been looking at some of the extra paraphernalia that men and women have adopted in order to maintain distance from the non-leisured classes. The exposure of garments that were not meant to be seen, and the leaving off of others altogether, represented a different aim, for here another of the threads of fashion comes into

58

play – the appeal of sexual display. Throughout the centuries this has been associated with real or imagined underclothing. In medieval and Renaissance times such garments were basic. In the last 250 years or so underclothing has been particularly important because during the greater part of the period the layers of outer and under clothing combined to create a shape that was very unlike a woman's natural form, leaving a male observer to imagine what was concealed. In a sense the aim is display in reverse.

The eighteenth-century woman was regarded as a creature of the chase, something of a coquette whose rustling silk brocades were a frivolous affectation of false modesty. So long as she felt confident about her undergarments she could afford to lie seductively in a hammock, or kick up her legs on the swing. The young lover in the Fragonard painting is clearly anxious for a glimpse of the forbidden regions of the girl's body. Off the swing, she could expose her chemise

by walking with her hoop tilted to one side and could also make sure that the decorative top of her chemise was visible above her corsage. The assumption was that to reveal portions of the underclothing was an erotic gesture symbolizing undressing. Some eighteenth-century fashions, such as the polonaise, which was fashionable between 1770 and 1785, exploited this idea to the extent of revealing the whole petticoat by tucking up the outer skirt in loops at the back. Earlier in the century an open robe was commonly worn which revealed· a long triangle of the petticoat at the front, from the waist to the hem. Often these petticoats were embroidered for extra richness, quilted for warmth and stiffness or were even more exoticly trimmed, like that of Marie Leszcynska, the Polish wife of Louis XV, who appeared sumptuously clad in an underskirt made entirely of ermine. But though the garment may have made a sexual appeal, Louis was not prevented from rushing to the more elusive charms

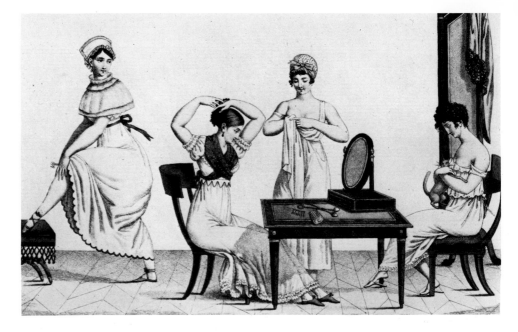

Right: This engraving of girls at their toilette in 1810 shows how Grecian statues influenced French costume at this time. The two girls on the right are seen in their underslips, the only garment worn beneath their flimsy dresses.

of Madame de Pompadour or Madame du Barry. Such overt displays of the undergarment for erotic appeal must surely have been subordinate to another function: like the slashed sleeves of medieval times, wealth was shown by one's ability to afford several layers of clothing.

Wealth, that god of the Victorian era, was responsible for the expanding petticoats that grew in number and bulk as the nineteenth century advanced, until the Victorian lady thought nothing of wearing four to six petticoats, one of them made of heavy red flannel. What better way could there be to avoid the pursuit of the vulgar than to put a physical distance between oneself and them by wearing voluminous skirts! If they copied, one had only to make one's skirt larger still until the enemy was forced to give in, for how could a young shop assistant hope to slide a vast skirt behind a counter? There was retribution for those who did. At a Staffordshire pottery £200 worth of goods were smashed in 1865 alone by the wide skirts of the workers. No doubt they were fined for the damage.

The expanding skirt expressed visually that woman was beginning to occupy a larger space in the social world, and that gentlemen must take note of her, if indeed they could get into the same room. In 1842, for instance, Lady Aylesbury was wearing '48 yards of material in each of her gowns and . . .a petticoat of down or feathers which

swells out this enormous expanse and floats like a vast cloud when she sits down or rises up,' as reported in the diary of Mrs Archer Clive. A bustle, a sausage-shaped piece of material, was usually tied round the waist, and multiple petticoats gave the required dome shape to the figure. Not everyone could afford swansdown: others were made of crinoline, literally horsehair (*crin*) and flaxcloth (*lin*). But when the cage crinoline hit the headlines in 1856 there was no stopping the working girl from assuming the fashions of her superiors. The cage crinoline was cheap. It was made of metal or whalebone hoops held together by tapes so that the skirt could hang over it in a smooth bell shape. On 18 July 1857 *The Times* reported that 40,000 tons of Swedish iron had been imported for the manufacture of crinolines: 'One Sheffield firm alone has taken an order for 40 tons of rolled steel for crinolines and a foreign order has been given for one ton a week for several weeks.'

The popularity of the crinoline waxed and waned with the fortunes of the Empress Eugénie, who had made it fashionable. She it was who persuaded Charles Frederick Worth, apparently against his better judgement, to promote it. When the Second Empire fell in 1870 and Eugénie fled, the crinoline suffered a setback, though it reappeared in 1881, when it was called a 'crinolette'. *Punch* expressed the general feeling prevalent at the time:

Who's responsible I ask you for this strange
   portentous birth
Of an ancient hideous fashion and an echo
   answers 'Worth'.
Store of steel they hold in Paris, and the
   maiden hearts may droop
We've to follow where they lead us and go
   back to wire and hoop.

It was Princess Alexandra, wife of the future King Edward VII, who made the crinolette unfashionable and the un-wired back bustle occupied the field for a decade.

In the twentieth century there has been only one period during which a substructure similar to the crinoline has been worn. This was in the 1950s, when the 'paper nylon party petticoat' produced a billowing knee-length skirt or a long skirt for evening wear. This fashion originated with Dior's New Look of 1947 but did not achieve general popularity until the petticoats became cheaper some years later.

Other forms of underwear – or *lingerie* as it has seductively been called from the Edwardian era onwards – had a more obvious erotic appeal than such fashion substructures, and figure largely in the wedding budget. Trousseaux consisted of dozens of everything: petticoats in flannel, linen, lawn and lace, combinations in silk or a silk and wool mixture, cotton drawers, two or three dozen nightdresses, usually profusely trimmed with ribbons and Valenciennes lace. 'Americans and other ultra-smart folk,' wrote the *Lady's Realm* in 1903, 'are very fond of black silk or gauze night-gowns, but... I confess a predilection for purest white .... You should spend a large portion of your trousseau money on these important garments.'

The American influence on the style of European underwear was marked. With the exception of the years of the Civil War, all cotton for underwear came from the Southern States, and during the war years Europeans and Northerners had to turn to the pre-viously more expensive linens and cambrics. When it ended, exponents of the Rational Dress movement were cam-paigning for more comfortable clothes and less underwear, for American girls led a more active life than their friends across the Atlantic, going for energetic walks and showing more interest in

sport. Gradually they threw away their corsets and began to discard some of their underclothing.

In England the American influence was reinforced by the scientific re-searches of Dr Jaeger from Stuttgart in Germany. His main tenet was that it was most healthy to wear plain, undyed wool next to the skin to absorb perspiration and to protect the outer clothing from becoming soiled. The croquet or tennis player was fast coming to realize that, indelicate as it might seem, a lady actual-ly did perspire as soon as she became more than a doll. Jaeger's underwear was so popular that shoppers descended on the London store in Regent Street in the 1880s, buying boxes of garments without even opening them until they got home. Men were particularly en-thusiastic advocates of the new 'sani-tary woollen underwear' and Ruskin, Oscar Wilde and Bernard Shaw were among Jaeger's chief supporters. Amer-ica, not to be left behind, produced a new species of undergarment knit double, the intervening spaces filled with saw-dust, the amount of which could be reduced or increased according to the weather. More widely adopted than this haybox type of garment was the singlet for men, who had previously been wear-ing buttoned vests.

But America's greatest contribution to the development of underwear has been in the discovery of new textiles. It was W.H. Carothers who in 1929 discovered nylon by accident when he was trying to make artificial rubber. He made it from coal, air, water and vegetable oils. In 1939 the first nylon stockings made their appearance, replacing the shiny silk stockings that had been covering women's legs since the twenties. Later developments made sweeping changes, so that it is now possible to wash and dry garments within a couple of hours and there is no need to iron them. The old functions of underwear – to protect the body from coarse dress materials, to keep one warm, to preserve class dis-tinctions and to disguise the human shape – no longer apply and *lingerie* today is designed mainly for comfort, though it also retains its erotic value.

Body Display

Erotic appeal is also an important facet

Above: A Jaeger advertise-ment tries to convince outsize ladies that they will be able to achieve the Edwardian S-shaped curve, with the 'Pauline' corset c. 1910.

Below: Dr Jaeger supporting his theory that all-wool garments were the most healthy. He is pictured in the 1880s wearing a wool stockinette tunic suit, a variation of the costumes he designed for the German army, which were tested to withstand the vagaries of weather.

of those garments that focus the observer's attention on certain parts of the body, shifting his gaze from beautiful shoulders to a well-formed bosom or a smooth back, swaying hips, lovely legs or a dainty ankle. The site of interest was always either above the waist or below it, never both, and the continual change from one area to another maintained the excitement. But whether the bosom or the legs have been exposed to public view, the part of the body that has been temptingly covered has almost always excited most interest. Thus Smollett's Roderick Random of his bride: 'Her bosom, through the veil of gauze that shaded it, afforded a prospect of Elysium.' Modesty itself, it seems, is part of sex attraction. It appears, too, in the demure costumes of the fourteenth and fifteenth centuries, when women draped huge folds of fabric over their abdomens and adopted a stance which

Above left: Ingres' portrait of Madame de Senonnes (1814) is rich in its depiction of jewelry.

Above: Watch and châtelaine in enamelled gold, made by Chapman of London (1781).

Left: A cigarette case and a sweet box made by Carl Fabergé in 1904. Both are enamelled gold and set with precious gems. The cigarette case bears the imperial cypher set in diamonds.

Opposite: Buttons such as these, had elaborate enamelled or painted designs. They dated from the 1780s in France and commonly showed portraits, fanciful scenes or patriotic slogans.

Above: The construction of the cage crinoline is seen in this Punch cartoon, and its impractability for everyday wear is satirized. The caption reads: 'Werry sorry 'm, but yer'l av' to leave yer krinerline outside.'

Below: The topless bathing fashions of the late sixties made the display of bare flesh fashionable off the beaches. Here, the model wears a chain bodice and miniskirt, slit at the thighs, from Rome's 1969 collections.

suggested pregnancy, thus indicating their fitness for the most supreme of feminine tasks. A more common indication of availability, which became immodest only in the coquette, was to uncover parts of the body that had previously been concealed. Thus the open ruff of the Elizabethans was left open partly for comfort, and partly to accentuate the *décolletage* of the dress. Some of the areas exposed strike us in the twentieth century as representing a curious notion of beauty, as for example the shaving of the head a good three inches back from the forehead indulged in by aristocratic ladies in Renaissance Italy. There is little doubt, however, that previous generations would have been much more shocked by the overt sexuality of today.

The flapper of the twenties was the first fashionable lady to reveal bare arms, shoulders, legs and even knees; yet strangely these displays had no erotic intention. The revealing nature of the flapper's clothes underlined her feeling of emancipation, her desire to create an impression of youthful carefreeness and assert her equality in a man's world by treating her body with unconcern. Many thought that she went too far in these attempts, since the overall result was to produce a totally unfeminine silhouette in which all her natural curves were reduced and flattened, leaving her with a figure like a tube. She may have been displaying parts of the body not seen in the streets before, but this was not for

sexual effect; her aim was rather to show men coming back from the wars that they would find a self-sufficient companion who was ready to take the place of friends they had lost.

In the thirties, when femininity had been somewhat restored, uncovering parts of the body was used by designers as a weapon in the sex game. It was in the early thirties that the back made one of its rare appearances as an area of interest. Evening dresses featured the new halter neckline, leaving the shoulders bare and exposing the back to the waist. Another style favoured the asymmetrical *décolletage*, with one shoulder covered with slight drapery, the other left bare. – a fashion revived in the seventies, when designers looked back to the thirties with nostalgia.

It was not until the sixties that styles swung once again to near-nudity. The teenagers born during the Second World War were growing up and were able to throw off the shackles of war sobriety that had hampered their parents. They initiated a return to youthfulness in clothing and the natural corollary was a tendency towards frank displays of physical charms. In the next decade the youth of Britain and America expressed their lust for life in a variety of clothes with cut-out or see-through details. Paper and cellophane dresses had a brief vogue in the mid-sixties, hinting alluringly that the body beneath was more important than an expendable frock that could be torn off. At the end of the decade, the garment *was* removed entirely and belles appeared at ultra-fashionable parties clad only in highly decorative body paint. Topless fashions first appeared in 1964, when daring women appeared in clothes resembling the costume of the Grecian snake goddess and in the south of France it became almost unfashionable to appear wearing a top to a bikini. With the mini-skirt of 1964–72 and the hot pants of 1971, the thigh became a centre of interest. Skin-tight sweaters further emphasized the shape of the nude figure without actually leaving it bare, though a tempting gap between the bottom of the sweater and the top of the skirt was often visible. Yet the modern girl does not have to follow the main trend of exposure in fashion if her legs are not her best

feature: fashion has turned full circle and long skirts can be seen as normal day wear. Tight clothes or cut away separates of every kind are available for her to display whichever part of her body she thinks most attractive. There has never been an age when freedom of self-expression in clothes, as in every other field of artistic interest, has been so much the keynote. In this respect the Women's Liberation Movement has had some influence, and although the majority of people laughed at their 'bra-burning' image, more and more young girls are discarding all ideas of foundation garments and underwear. Self-conscious display has reached its peak in leaving the way open for each individual to choose her own silhouette. It leads to a social distinction of a novel kind, based not on rank and wealth but on the assertion of physical endowments combined with taste. The old aim of trying to outshine one's contemporaries is still there. It is the main reason today why we have still not chosen to wear Plato's uniform toga.

Above left: A 'flapper' in 1928, her arms and legs the only relief from the tube-like shape. A boyish stance is also adopted.

Above centre: Lady Sylvia Ashley, (later Mrs Douglas Fairbanks), wearing an elegant version of the bare-back dress in 1934.

Above right: Mini skirt and silver stockings display the woman's figure, whose curves are offset by the metallic lustre. Dress by Emmanuelle Khanh (1969–70), one of the leading ready-to-wear designers of the sixties.

Left: The 'hot pants' fashion of 1971 brought the thighs into focus as an area of erotic interest. The longer leg was almost always covered by boots. In this outfit the bust is also emphasized by the patch pockets in the jumper, and a tough 'I-can-defend-myself' image is created by cartridge belt.

Chapter Four

Trousers and Sports Clothes

Who Wears the Trousers?

The ideal picture of the married couple in Victorian times would feature a demure young lady looking feminine and fragile despite her voluminous skirts, and a sombrely dressed man towering protectively above her, his top hat exaggerating his dominating air. Most women were content with their role of subjection to the will of man, in spite of a growing awareness among intellectuals of the inequality of their position. The idea of raising the status of women seems to have begun with the French Revolution and, in England, with the publication in 1792 of Mary Wollstonecraft's book *A Vindication of .the Rights of Women*; but it was not until the 1850s that a man, the Englishman John Stuart Mill, paid any significant attention to the problem. Mill asked questions in Parliament and encouraged a movement for women's suffrage that was to grow slowly through the rest of the nineteenth and early twentieth centuries. The United States, leading the way, granted the vote to women in 1920, but women in Britain had to wait until 1928 to be granted full adult suffrage. In France, meanwhile, the problem was not faced until much later, with women gaining the vote only in 1944 and in Switzerland total female suffrage was not achieved until this decade.

The struggle for political and social equality was expressed in fashion by a tendency to borrow male garments for female clothing. Thus the man's shirt became a tunic dress, his collar and tie

became a blouse with jabot and his jacket was transformed into the tailor-made suit. But above all it was his trousers, the symbol of physical freedom, that women began to adopt and adapt with increasing confidence until they became respectable and fashionable wear for all occasions. This has happened only in the last fifty years, for a mood of prudery prevailed throughout the nineteenth century, when trousers were singled out for secretive speculation. No self-respecting lady could even mention the word and women had to refer to trousers as 'inexpressibles' or 'a pair of dittoes'. As early as 1836–7, when Dickens's *Oliver Twist* was being published, it seems to have been polite to avoid the horrid word:

'I tossed off the clothes; got softly out of bed; drew on a pair of – '

'Ladies present, Mr. Giles,' murmured the tinker.

'– of shoes, sir,' said Mr. Giles, laying great emphasis on the word.

Later in the decade this delicacy went to such extremes that even piano legs were covered up, and any hint of anatomical curves in men's legs was quickly disguised in a pair of tube-like garments.

This is where the history of trousers, as opposed to the hose, breeches and pantaloons of previous centuries, begins. The first stage in the metamorphosis was the loose trousers like pantaloons worn by the *sans culottes* (literally 'without breeches'), the nickname for the French revolutionaries. (Loose, short

Opposite: Napoleon I who considered himself the arbiter of taste in costume, dressed with enormous care. In this portrait by Ingres he wears a velvet coat, knee breeches and silk stockings.

Below: A Parisian 'sans-culottes' during the French Revolution, wearing the striped trousers which later climbed into the realm of high fashion. These trousers were originally anti-dress, rejecting the tight body-revealing breeches of the aristocracy.

pleated at the waist and fitted at the ankles.

Trousers were noticeably slow to find universal acceptance, as this story from the dandified Captain Gronow's *Reminiscences* of 1816 illustrates: 'As I went out a great deal into the world and was every night at some ball or party, I found that knee breeches were only worn by a few old fogies; trousers and shoes being the usual costume of all young men of the day....' But when he ventured to appear at a party at Manchester House given by the Prince Regent's current mistress, Lady Hertford, Horace Seymour tapped him on the shoulder and said: 'The "great man" [meaning the prince] is very much surprised that you should have ventured to appear in his presence without knee-breeches. He considers it as a want of proper respect for him.' But in less than a month Captain Gronow had the satisfaction of seeing the Prince himself appear at a ball in trousers.

In mid-century, trousers were popularly brightly coloured with a stripe down the seam or had a check or plaid design. Queen Victoria and Prince Albert were responsible for the popularity of tartans – the one fashion they initiated – for their retreat at Balmoral was crammed full of tartan weaves of all clans, including the Balmoral tartan. This had

Above: Knee breeches, worn before trousers became fashionable. The picture shows a man of fashion of 1700 talking to his counterpart in 1800.

Right: Painting by James Tissot of Lord Carlingford wearing slim-line trousers, probably the 'American trouser', held closely to the waist with tight buttons over the pockets (c. 1860–80).

trousers had been worn by working men and it was these who formed the mass of revolutionaries). These did indeed represent a breakaway from the knee-breeches and elaborate buckles of the 'aristos', but they only heralded the advent of the trouser proper, since immediately after the Revolution men's pantaloons tightened into sex-display garments not unlike the medieval and Renaissance hose criticized by Chaucer's parson. Young boys in the last quarter of the eighteenth century were wearing looser pantaloons, but it was not until 1814 that trousers emerged, aided by the taste for things Cossack that followed Napoleon's campaign in Russia and the Czar's visit to London in 1814. 'cossacks', as they were called, were very full and were gathered in at the waist and round the ankles. But this style was distinctly cumbersome and by 1820 cossacks were further modified, being

Left: Men's fashions in 1924: racing outfits, golf and morning suits. The male mannequins were a novelty, and male modelling did not become a profession until 1950.

been designed by the Prince Consort himself and was black, red and lavender on a grey background. Warehouses opened up in London and tartan became all the rage in Paris. A clerk in one of the tartan offices was responsible, through a mis-spelling, for giving tweed its name: the characteristic cloth woven in the border country was called 'tweel' (Scottish for 'twill'), but the clerk carelessly substituted a 'd' for the 'l'. Since at the time Sir Walter Scott's novels, which indeed centred on the banks of the Tweed, were enjoying renewed popularity, the new word seemed ideal for promoting Scottish twill. Tweeds were available in checks as well as tartans and were very popular for men's trousers, especially for the baggy 'peg-top' style that came into fashion in 1857.

Peg-tops were wide at the hips and gradually sloped inwards to fit close at the ankles. They were not universally worn and were often associated with the type of man who adopted the drooping whiskers worn by Lord Dundreary in Tom Taylor's comedy *Our American Cousin*. The fashion for these trousers lasted until 1865, when they were replaced by the 'American trouser'. These were narrow at the hips, were held close into the waist by a belt and buckle instead of braces or suspenders,

and had a slight flare at the bottom. They were designed for elegant wear, while in the country the trouser shape reverted to a hint of the earlier knee-breeches. Trousers with long spats or garters buttoning up to the knee were worn for hunting or walking, though in 1863 baggy knickerbockers – a fashion taken from the Rifle Volunteers – began to be worn.

The same styles for men's trousers continued, with slight modifications of cut, into the twentieth century. By 1925 the narrow, elegant cut of the Edwardian era had disappeared with the introduction of wide trousers known as Oxford bags and baggy knickerbockers called plus-fours. Oxford bags proper had only a brief vogue but they continued to influence the basic shape of trousers, which remained wide and tubular. This unflattering fashion, though scorned by youthful dandies, was not finally superseded until the 1960s, when well-cut, close-fitting trousers became the dress of most men.

Women's trousers

Most styles of men's trousers sooner or later found a parallel in women's wear. Thus pantaloons or drawers were worn under the cage crinoline from the 1860s onwards, as were on occasion tartan or brightly coloured knickerbockers. For

Below: Amelia Jenks Bloomer, pioneer of the Rational Dress Campaign, launched the 'Bloomer costume' in 1849. The garment was a cross between 'cossack' trousers and long knickerbockers worn with a loose overskirt, and the whole effect was reminiscent of harem dress.

Below: At several stages throughout history European ladies have absorbed influences from various different cultures. Travel tales in the first half of the 19th century provoked a vogue for fancy dress, and paintings, such as this group of ladies in Algeria by Delacroix captured the mood.

all the attention that was lavished on such undergarments, they were not in fact intended to be seen, so that when the elegant Duchess of Manchester caught her hoops while climbing over a stile and landed upside down, displaying a pair of scarlet knickerbockers to the world, the Duc de Malakoff remarked, *'C'était diabolique!'* Pantaloons and knickerbockers have shrunk both in size and in name to our modern panties or knickers. It is somewhat surprising to note that they began life as borrowings from the male wardrobe.

The first time trousers are reported to have made an appearance as an outer garment for women in England was when the Duchess of Montrose appeared

at a shooting party in 1847 wearing plaid trousers beneath a calf-length skirt-petticoat. But the Duchess was an individualist and there is no evidence to suggest that she knew of the movement towards a similar style of dress that was taking place across the Atlantic. It was indeed in America that trousers really made their début, when Amelia Jenks Bloomer launched the Rational Dress Campaign in 1849 by appearing in a garment that was a cross between a pair of cossacks and long knickerbockers, with a short skirt modestly worn over the top as a concession to convention. The 'Bloomer costume' crossed over to Britain in 1851, but made very little impact, except in Belfast, where the local

Above: The Rendezvous, coloured engraving of a country scene by Guérard. The horseman is wearing trousers with strapped instep. The artist portrays him with the small feet thought elegant at the time (mid-18th century).

Left: Members of the Wilson family grouped round a memorial to William Pitt the Younger, painted by John Downman (late 18th century). Three of the gentlemen are wearing buckskin breeches and the fourth is formally dressed in black velvet.

papers noted with astonishment 'three females' – wife and daughters of a sea captain – promenading in public in this new-fangled garment.

Bloomers had only a limited success even in America, though the redoubtable Amelia toured the country lecturing women on their virtues for many years. They were clearly ahead of their time, as it was not until thirty years later that the Rational Dress Campaign won any real victories. By this time women had become more interested in sport and had discovered that crinoline skirts and bustles were very inconvenient for their new activities. Bicycling and tricycling were the particular favourites of the 1880s, with the result that when the divided skirt was again paraded at the Rational Dress Show of 1883 bloomers

a new idea even in dress.

'Ever since the Bloomer costume, however the idea has been gaining in popularity, although but slowly, and at the Health Exhibition at South Kensington several divided dresses of the most pronounced type were shown and met with favourable comment.'

Among those who favoured the garment was the 'new woman', the college girl recently accepted at Cambridge University. For her the great attraction of bicycling was that she could go out for rides with gentlemen unaccompanied, for what chaperone would allow herself to be induced to mount two wheels. Besides it was good to feel free, as the 'new woman' in Marie Corelli's novel *Mrs Maddenham*, published in

Right: The Bloomer costume styled for party occasions (1851-9). The gentlemen are wearing trousers that are held down by a strap under the instep.

were immediately seized upon as suitable bicycling wear. In 1885 the American Mrs Ada Ballin published a book called *The Science of Dress*, in which she attempted to explain the failure of bloomers thirty years before:

The feeling against the Bloomer costume was very strong for although it had many good points about it, it represented too violent a change from the fashion of the time and ladies would not adopt it for fear of appearing ridiculous. Reform to be effective must be gradual, and it takes some time for the public to become accustomed to

1897, says: '...all the best set bike; a woman's legs have never had fair play till now. What are legs for I should like to know? We've had to hide them under long skirts for ages except on the stage. It's time they should see day light.' But the novel's ladylike heroine 'shivered [at these words] as though a douche of cold water had been poured down her back, then blushed deeply as though scalding wine had been poured down her throat.' However, a girl of such acute sensibilities was on the losing side, and by the time she was a grandmother she was destined to see girls skimming by on

TROUSERS FOR WOMEN ARE NOT NECESSARILY UNATTRACTIVE. THEY CAN BE QUITE BECOMING IN THE FORM OF—

A SMOKING SUIT—

AND FOR SPORTS WEAR THEY ARE NOT UNREASONABLE;

BUT SHOULD THEY BE ADOPTED IN THE CITY—

IN THE DOMESTIC CIRCLE—

AT ASCOT—

FOR DINNER-PARTIES—

OR IN THE BALLROOM—

OLD-FASHIONED PEOPLE MAY REGRET THE MORE MAIDENLY FASHIONS OF TO-DAY—

OR EVEN THOSE OF A DOZEN YEARS AGO.

Above: Slacks in 1932. They were still called pyjamas at this time and were worn for home lounging.

Left: Punch's *comments on trousers (1927).*

Below: Mr Freeman was the 'pop art' clothing designer of the early seventies and he specialized in creating fun clothes that were meant to be laughed at.

bicycles wearing nothing but the briefest shorts.

Trousers or bloomers were not much worn at home, except in the fancy-dress form of what people imagined an Arabian princess might wear. Lady Mary Wortley Montagu had seen a real princess on her embassy to Constantinople in 1717:

She wore a vest called *donalma,* and which differs from a *caftán* by longer sleeves, and folding over at the bottom. It was of purple cloth, strait to her shape, and thick set on each side, down to her feet, and round the sleeves.... This habit was tied, at the waist, with two large tassels of smaller pearl, and round the arms embroidered with large diamonds: her shift fastened at the bottom with a great diamond, shaped like a lozenge; her girdle as broad as the broadest English ribbon, entirely covered with diamonds.

A century and a half later this costume had been embellished in people's imaginations and the long shift became a pair of loose flowing trousers, clasped with precious gems at the ankle. A wave of enthusiasm for the Orient was initiated by the publication in 1885 of Sir Richard

Burton's translation of *A Thousand Nights and a Night* and by other exotic tales that followed it. Ballet designers like Bakst and Erté in the first and second decades of the twentieth century made full use of the inspiration of the East and many of their costumes had richly decorative divided skirts. This had repercussions on fashion when a brief vogue for the 'harem skirt' for evening wear achieved limited popularity in 1910. Then in 1921, when Rudolph Valentino stirred millions of hearts by his performance as the romantic Arab in the film *The Sheik,* quasi-eastern dress was promptly adopted by his devoted admirers.

In the 1920s trousers became an accepted item of women's wear. Munitions workers had worn trousers for comfort under their long overalls and once the war was over they were not anxious to relinquish this convenient garment. At first trousers were worn secretively in the safety of the home as 'leisure pyjamas', becoming a respectable form of clothing for receiving afternoon guests in one's boudoir. Pyjamas were also worn on the beach and the year 1928–9 saw a popular vogue for pyjama parties. These were not bedtime romps, as the name might suggest, since pyjamas were not yet specifically thought of as nightwear; a pyjama party indicated that economy of dress and type of entertainment, was to be the style and guests must expect to be regaled with such inelegant delights as beer and sausages and mash. With the world situation creeping towards the great economic depression, a party on this basis was very welcome. Pyjamas worn at these occasions were, however, highly decorative and showed no signs

Above: The casual wear of the mid-19th century is seen again in Gustave Courbet's painting, Bonjour M. Courbet. *The artist's peasant-style clothing contrasts sharply with that of his two friends who are out for a country walk in town dress, complete with hats, white gloves and canes.*

Opposite: Parasols were uncommon for men and the man in this painting by Claude Monet carries an umbrella to shade him from the sun. He is dressed to conform to the image of the gentleman artist of the late 19th century.

of economy with their inset stripes, scalloped edges, fancy buttons and bell bottoms. They were made of lace, crêpe de chine or a wool mixture.

Pyjamas, not called slacks for women until about 1936, suited the bachelor-girl image that the postwar woman was trying to promote. Now that she was dressed like a man she could lead a life no less active than his and hope to be accepted as his equal. There was even a fad in 1926 for women to wear dinner jackets in the evening, like men, though they did wear them with a tailored skirt. Marlene Dietrich wore her own version of an evening trouser suit, but

The blue jeans worn during the next three decades were an anti-fashion phenomenon, surpassed only by the gimmicky 'hot pants' (sports shorts by another name) popularized in 1971 by British pop designer Mr Freedom.

Sports clothes

Strangely enough, trousers for sports wear began to make an appearance only in the twenties and they were by no means accepted wear. Right up until the end of the thirties women golfers were cutting a most inelegant figure in crumpled pullovers, shapeless skirts and de-

Above: The Rev. Robert Walker skating on Duddingston Loch, *by Sir Henry Raeburn (mid-18th century). The skates are simply tied over his ordinary walking shoes.*

Above right: Skating was popular whenever women's skirts allowed the freedom of movement required. Here women of 1869 are seen on the pond wearing outdoor clothing. Muffs and fur-trimmed hats and jackets were typical winter accessories.

it was left to Twiggy in 1968 to appear in a dinner jacket and trousers complete with bow tie. The dinner-jacket or tuxedo craze was an extreme, but in such exaggerations women were merely groping their way towards liberty, not only exerting their right to freedom of movement, but also throwing off slavishness to fashion conventions. Ogden Nash, while appreciating the freedom American women were seeking, had this to say about trousers in the 1940s:

Sure, deck your lower limbs in pants;
Yours are the limbs, my sweeting
You look divine as you advance –
Have you seen yourself retreating?

plorably dowdy shoes and hats. They probably avoided trousers because without them it was possible to dress once for the whole day: the country woman could fling on a coat for a morning's walk, lunch with a friend, rush down to the golf club for a quick game and then tear back again to a cocktail party without looking unsuitably clad. This was a great advance on the previous decades, when it was still necessary to change from morning dress to afternoon gown, to tea gown to evening gown, carefully adjusting the skirt length at each change. In her autobiography Elinor Glyn describes the ritual English country weekends in Edwardian times:

Left: The Cathcart family in 1784-5; painting by David Allen. The gentlemen are dressed for cricket and are wearing waistcoats and knee-breeches. The children are clothed in silks and satins ill-suited to the activities of childhood.

It was not correct to lunch in tweeds and ladies were expected to change into a frock. After lunch they changed back again into tweeds if it was a shooting party, or put on a full length sealskin coat if they were to go motoring. For tea they changed back again into tea-gowns, seductive diaphanous affairs with low-cut bodices, while the men wore brightly coloured velvet smoking suits: sapphire blue, emerald green, crimson. For dinner they wore full evening dress, the men in white ties and tails and the women in dresses with trains, carrying ostrich feather fans.

It would be misleading to give the impression that the eighteenth- and early nineteenth-century girl was totally inactive, but sport as a feature of the young lady's repertoire of accomplishments achieved popularity only in the latter half of the nineteenth century, originating as a breath of fresh air from the United States. For many years, however, there was little concession to ease and comfort. Ordinary costume restricted women's movements and it was not until 1865 that a croquet dress was deliberately designed to ensure that they would not tear it if they aimed for a good shot; previously women had simply worn their garden-party dresses for croquet or for tennis. Croquet outfits were usually made of muslin and worn over a coloured petticoat, the sleeves were unlined and made of a series of light puffs and ribbons. The skirt, almost always white, was looped up to display a shorter coloured petticoat, much like the eighteenth-century polonaise. A similar dress was worn for other ladies' sports, such as tennis, archery and ice

Left: Lady cricketers wearing tight jacket bodices over slightly padded skirts (1779), and slanted bonnets protecting their high hairstyles.

or roller skating. Though 'rinking', as skating was known at the time, was very popular, it was completely dependent on current fashion trends; thus when skirts grew tighter in the 1870s and 1880s it was quite impossible to skate and the activity was temporarily abandoned, until Edwardian styles made it possible again. Besides being popular in itself (again one suspects the attractions of escaping the watchful eye of the chaperone) rinking gave opportunities for displaying elegant clothing. The best-dressed women wore garments elegantly trimmed with fur, fur muffs and a small fur hat, or an ermine waistcoat for the extravagant.

Men, too, wore their ordinary day clothes for skating, as well as for cricket, where their only concession to the demands of the game was to discard their outer garments. But since cricket was a team game some kind of uniformity of clothing began to be necessary for display matches and captains encouraged their teams to adopt some common feature in their dress – perhaps gold or silver bindings on their tricorne hats or

Opposite: Bicyclists sporting the Bloomer costume in the Bois de Boulogne, Paris. Painting by Jean Béraud, c. 1900.

Below left: Twiggy made the slender masculine style figure into every teenager's ideal. Here she wears full male evening dress (1968), the ultimate in unisex.

Below right: Miss Sweden (1971) displaying her figure and sporting vitality in hot pants, tights, fancy thread-needle shoes and fake fur.

79

a blue coat with gilt buttons. In 1787, a few years after its formation, the famous Marylebone Cricket Club in London adopted sky-blue dress for its teams. White did not become the standard dress for cricketers until the 1850s and the wearing of cricket pads was not general practice before the 1840s.

Cricket was not simply a man's sport, however. Women had been playing since 1745 or thereabouts, with their skirts tucked up to make them a little shorter, though this was the sole concession to utility. Mrs Ada Ballin in *The Science of Dress* pointed to other needs

was tied round the waist with a sash. The material was usually navy-blue serge and a pair of matching knickers was worn underneath. The name 'bloomers' came to be applied to this shrunken version of the original garment. Comfort was thus at last setting a fashion of its own, though only in the schools, where it lasted as standard uniform for more than seventy years.

Tennis was another energetic game for which no adequate clothing had been devised. How the ladies of the Victorian and Edwardian eras managed to serve or run for the ball in their stiff corseted

Above: Suzanne Lenglen was the belle of the tennis courts in the twenties and was dressed by the Paris couturier, Patou. She popularized the wearing of the bandeau which became the hallmark of the twenties' image. The picture was taken in 1945.

Above right: Alice Marble astonished Wimbledon by appearing in shorts in 1932, though this more convenient garb was worn throughout the later thirties and forties.

when she suggested that girl cricketers ought to have a bosom pad tucked between their dress and undergarment to 'prevent any harm which might possibly arise from a chance blow from a cricket ball'. Needless to say she also recommended bloomers as eminently suitable for so active a game, but these continued to be worn only by schoolgirls and Mrs Ballin was unable to persuade women to accept them. It was left to a Swedish gymnastics teacher, Madame Bergman Osterberg, who introduced a gym tunic for physical training in schools in 1885, to continue the good work. Her outfit was knee length and sleeveless and was worn with a plain blouse; it had three box pleats in the front and at the back, so that movement was unrestricted, and

clothes is something of a mystery. Yet when in 1922 Suzanne Lenglen appeared at Wimbledon in a 'short' skirt the general public was shocked. Mrs Lenglen, who was the then prima donna of the tennis world, was nothing if not practical and also wore a bandeau to keep her hair off her face, thus initiating a new fashion gimmick. So characteristic is this style of a whole era that in 1972 a man's shirt appeared printed all over with Gloria Swanson, in her bandeau, as a tribute to the twenties. Yet if Suzanne Lenglen caused a stir, this was nothing to the sensation Alice Marble produced when she appeared on court in 1932 wearing white shorts. This was thought by many people to be going really too far for the sake of the game.

What would they have said if they could have seen 'Gorgeous Gussie' leaping into the air in 1949 to display lace-edged frilly panties beneath her diminutive tennis skirt!

Unisex

The history of trousers is in itself a comment on prevailing sexual attitudes and one of the most significant developments of the twentieth century has been the movement towards unisex garments, clothes that can be worn by both sexes. In political and economic terms women

are to a greater extent 'wearing the trousers', or at least proclaiming their right to compete with men on equal terms. But what of their sexual role? In our so-called permissive society sexual matters are discussed with greater freedom, and both the Women's Liberation Movement and the open discussions of homosexuality and transvestism indicate an awareness of the complexity of sexual roles. The versatility of modern dress design enables the individual to reveal himself, through his dress, as he really is – in a bewildering number of ways.

Unisex is perhaps a reaction to this complexity, for on the surface it is an elimination of dress as a sexual bait. Women have drawn closer to men and

men to women, though it is significant that men do not yet wear skirts! The unisex outfit, first seen in the collection of Newman of Paris in 1966, consists of close-fitting levi trousers, also called jeans, with a front fly zip for both men and women, jumpers, shirts and shirt blouses, cravats or scarves, sports tops and soft shoes. The movement was popularized in Britain when Harrod's opened its new 'Way In' boutique in London in 1967, which was one of the first to be designed for the young couple shopping together. Since then the idea has spread across the Atlantic to America and back to France, where it originated.

The unisex trend in clothes is perhaps the nearest fashions have come in modern times to the Platonic ideal of costume, for though the shapeless toga is still scorned, now at last we have men and women submerging sexual and class differences in their choice of apparel. Yet though the influence of unisex on fashion is marked, it is not, and doubtless never will be, the uniform of a wide sector of society. It is essentially a youthful fashion, since normally only young female bodies can have pretentions towards boyishness. Sooner or later, as marriage or motherhood make a woman's sexual role clearer, a tendency towards more feminine outlines is inevitable. This can be compatible with the wearing of trousers: from 1971 onwards there was a vogue in most of Europe and the United States – perhaps not a lasting one – for wearing soft feminine smocks over jeans. This gives women an ambiguous air of looking as if they might be pregnant, thus emphasizing their feminine attributes and pointing in a direction where the unisex movement, for all its democratic appeal, cannot follow.

Left: By 1970 even a traditional store like Burberry's of London had succumbed to the influence of Unisex on clothing. The two models sport double-breasted coats and gangster style hats.

Below: Unisex proper shows his/hers outfits that are exactly the same in every detail. Denim suits like this 1968 version were particularly adaptable to male and female figures.

Chapter Five

Dandies and Spivs

The great dandies were men with enough wealth to wear finery of an opulence beyond the reach of other men: Lorenzo il Magnifico, for example, with his velvet, fur-lined robes, or François I and Henry VIII, who wore embroidered cloth of gold doublets and massive slashed sleeves, or Charles I's favourite, the Duke of Buckingham, who had strings of diamonds loosely sewn to his clothes so that he could break the thread and scatter them among his fellows, looking on from his superior position as they stooped to save the precious gems. They were men who dressed to look decorative, the prime motive of the dandy. Throughout the eighteenth century the love of finery continued to be indulged in a more modified form (except at court, and especially the French court, where one courtier was still set against another in an attempt to be the most splendidly attired) but it was not until the nineteenth century that a new concept of discreet elegance replaced the idea that a dandy must be as conspicuous as possible.

The Eighteenth Century

The beaux, fops and dandies of the eighteenth century were men who overloaded themselves with clothes – layer upon layer of lace ruffles, gold embroidery, ostentatious knee buckles, shoes with outsize rosettes and red heels. They wore powder, patches and perfume and carried nosegays to keep evil odours away. These effeminate creatures were much mocked in the dramas of the day. Charles Coffey in *The Female Parson*

(1730) gives this picture of a beau:

With snuff-box, powder'd wig and arms akimbo
Cane, ruffles, sword-knot, burdash hat and Feather,
Perfume, fine essence, brought from Lord knows whither.

The fashionable beau was a colourful spectacle. 'A black velvet coat, a green and silver waistcoat, yellow velvet breeches, and blue stockings' was how the dress of one gentleman was described in the journal the *Inspector* in 1751. Certainly he would be very particular about the colour and the fit of his clothes, like the country squire Henry Purefoy, who was always writing to his local tailor asking for news of the latest town styles and specifying his requirements in minute detail when he ordered his frocks, waistcoats and breeches. A good example of this is a letter from him dated 11 May 1736: 'The Gold laced wastcoat you made mee last year has done you no credit in the making, it gapes so intolerably before at the bottom, when I button it at ye wastbone of my breetches & stand upright it gapes at the bottom beyond my breetches & everybody takes notice of it. As to my size I am partly the same bignesse as I was when in Town last, but you made the last cloaths a little too streight.'

When King George III came to the throne of England in 1760 as a young man of only 22, a breath of fresh air entered men's fashions generally, re-

Opposite: Regency à la Mode, *etching by William Heath (1812) satirizing a dandy preparing his toilet. Rouge and skin lotions were commonly used in spite of the poisons they contained, and the discomfort of tight corsetting was suffered even by those whose figures could not be saved.*

Below: Dandified clothing at the court of Louis XVI in the mid-18th century shows how competitive court dressing had become. Accessories include satin rosettes at the knee, wrist and on the shoes, lace ruffling, jewelled sword hilt and orders of honour. Painting by Nattier.

Above: A macaroni in 1773. The nosegay, the rosettes and tiny hat are all typical elements of the costume, though exaggerated here of course.

placing the stuffiness of the old Germanic court. High-born dandies called themselves 'beaux', 'bloods' and 'bucks' and sought to distinguish themselves from their baser imitators, who were known as 'jessamies', 'dappers', 'smarts' and 'sparks'. The apparel of each of these classes of dandy – and the difference between them was felt to be very important – had some nicety that distinguished it from the others, though at this distance of time we may find it hard to spot precisely what set a dapper apart from a smart. It may have been simply a scalloped shoe tongue or a rosette in the tricorne hat.

During the early part of George III's reign the display of fine clothes was encouraged. Clive's victory at Plassey in 1757 had assured the British hold on India and administrators returning home laden with jewels and damasks were cutting a figure as wealthy nabobs. Clive himself set a fashion for spangled or tinselled suits by appearing at a ball in a glitter of diamonds.

In contrast to this brash vulgarity, a new club was formed in 1764 by the Grand Tour *cognoscenti*, who affected extreme sensibility and an effeminate style of dress. They were known as 'macaronis' and they soon made the Italian dish of that name, a speciality at the Macaroni Club, the fashionable fare of the travelled gentry. Journalists were scornful and in 1772 the *Town and Country Magazine* described them thus:

'They make a most ridiculous figure with hats an inch in the brim that do not cover but lie upon the head with about two pounds of fictitious hair formed into what is called a 'club' hanging down their shoulders. The end of the skirt of their coat reaches the first button of their breeches which are either brown-striped or white; their coat sleeves are so tight that they can with difficulty get their arms through their cuffs.... Their legs are covered all colours of the rainbow. Their shoes are scarce slippers and their buckles are within an inch of the toe. Such a figure, essenced and perfumed, with a bunch of lace sticking out under its chin, puzzles the common passenger to determine the thing's sex.'

With this outfit the macaronis wore two watches, the first presumably for telling what the time was, the other for telling what it was not! Yet, ridiculous as their costume may have been, it did have one lasting effect. The flaps of their pockets were so long that they had great difficulty in reaching their handkerchiefs. This delicate problem was solved by the addition of an inside pocket, which has remained a feature of men's jackets to this day.

The influence of the macaronis was so far-reaching that the extravagances of their dress were even adopted by young lawyers and doctors. Thus there

Right: 'Merveilleuses' and 'incroyables' in the 1790s. Both men and women wear high, throat-constricting cravat knots, large earrings and absurd hats. Striped clothes were very popular.

84

Far left: George IV as Prince of Wales in 1792. Though corpulent, he was still only thirty years old and fancied himself as a dandy.

Left: A young dandy exhibiting the excesses of the cravat craze (1819).

Below: 'Going to White's', the dandy club; engraving by Richard Dighton (1819). One of the dandy images through the centuries has been to exhibit tough substantiality, which this illustration conveys. Henry VIII's clothing in the 16th century showed the same concern.

were macaroni barristers, doctors and clergymen and even macaroni Quakers. A young fellow was nothing without a 'toothpick between his teeth and his knuckles crammed into his coat-pocket'. The macaroni costume even crossed the Atlantic to America, where 'Yankee Doodle stuck a feather in his cap and called it macaroni'.

Similar to the macaronis were the French *incroyables* of the 1790s, who copied the English dandies by dressing in a curious mixture of fashionable fantasy garments and English country clothes. The *incroyable* truly was, as his name suggests, incredible. He walked the streets in the most amazing combinations of garish stripes, favouring bright colours as a living celebration of the end of the Revolution and the *ancien régime.* The stripes were horizontal or vertical, or preferably the two together. The tails of his riding-coat were so long that they almost touched the ground, his waistcoat was so short that it hardly covered his chest and his neckcloth was wrapped round so many times that it formed a kind of pedestal on which his face rested. His hair, like that of his female counterpart, the *merveilleuse,* was studiedly dishevelled and he wore on top of it an odd crescent moon-shaped hat that must have presented a bizarre appearance.

But such exaggerated fashions were not typical of the ordinary French male and were not copied elsewhere. They were adopted only by a select group of narcissists who could afford to patronize the ailing fashion industry in France, drifting, like their counterparts in England and America, from one fashion gimmick to another throughout the last years of the late eighteenth century. What they needed was a leader who could dictate a standard of elegance. That man was Beau Brummell.

Dandy Classicism

George Brummell, the grandson of a valet, was born in 1778; he learned from his father to care for his clothes and from his surroundings how to behave in genteel society. His father died a relatively wealthy man, leaving his son £1,500 a year – not a fortune but a respectable sum that should have enabled him to lead a life of leisure and pleasure as only a dandy knew how. Brummell's downfall was caused by one of those pleasures, gambling, to which he was addicted as firmly as to a drug. It was this that led to the dissipation of his fortune and he ended his days in penury in the French town of Caen. But during his day of glory, from about 1795 to 1813, he was, in his way, as absolute a monarch as

Above: The striped waist-coats and trousers in this etching by William Heath (1822) were throught very stylish, as were the yellow breeches.

Below: Although Beau Brummell was the arbiter of men's fashions, no good portraits of him exist. This engraving after a contemporary miniature shows him wearing one of the cravat knots on which he expended hours of his time.

Louis XIV. In the matter of clothes he had complete power over the future George IV, who is said to have burst into tears when Brummell told him that his breeches did not fit. But for one fatal day on which Brummell made a joke at the expense of the prince's mistress (and unofficial wife), Mrs Fitzherbert, he might have stayed to enjoy the fruits of his influence in the splendour of the court. Unfortunately the prince never forgave him.

Nevertheless it was the Prince of Wales's patronage that established Brummell in society. He frequented all the dandy clubs in London such as Arthur's, Almack's, Boodle's, Watier's and White's. The last two were his favourites and he was to be found at one or other most evenings. In between whiles he would put in an appearance at the opera or at a *soirée*. His maxim was to stay until he had made an impression and then leave. His attitude towards his personal relationships was the same as his view on clothing: elegant effect was all that was needed. Clothes must be subdued, clean and well cut. A gentleman need not display his aristocracy on his

sleeve, but in his manner and attention to detail. Cleanliness for Beau Brummell was almost a fetish. He would bathe three times a day, polish his boots with a secret mixture (said to contain champagne), and send his linen daily to the country to be washed. Some of his French imitators went so far as to send their laundry all the way from Paris to be washed in the English countryside, and doubtless American dandies would have followed suit had not the expense been prohibitive.

The more puritanical among Americans had, however, been aware of the value of cleanliness long before Beau Brummell was born. George Washington, who had once himself been an enthusiastic dandy, found time in 1776, in the midst of the Revolutionary Wars, to write to his nephew, George Steptoe Washington:

Decency and cleanliness will always be the first objects in the dress of a judicious and sensible man. A conformity to the prevailing fashion in a certain degree is necessary – but it does not follow from thence that a man should always get a new coat, or other clothes, upon every trifling change in the

Above: Benjamin Disraeli as a young blood, after Daniel Maclise (1820s). He was fond of wearing extravagant finger rings, a fashion that was not copied.

Above right: Alfred d'Orsay in 1834, by Daniel Maclise. The drawing gives him tiny feet which were thought very elegant and many dandies squeezed into shoes several sizes too small to achieve this effect.

Right: Two French dandies in 1839, equivalents of the English 'swells'. Fat cigars were carried as an accessory to the image rather than for the pleasure they afforded.

Previous page: Portrait of Monsieur Cadet by Pierre Prudhon (end of the 18th century). His costume exhibits a preoccupation with buttons common in dandified clothing.

mode, when, perhaps, he has two or three very good ones by him.

Visible linen in particular had to be spotlessly clean and well starched. The cravat, which was called a dicky by New Englanders, was the mark of a dandy's skill and became something of a fetish. It was a large square of linen, muslin or silk folded diagonally into a band and starched to the texture of fine writing paper. It was wound round the collar and attached to the shirt with a single solitaire pin, the top of the collar appearing above it to hold the throat rigid and give that look of blasé indifference characteristic of the dandy. When Brummell first appeared in a stiffened cravat, says *The English Spy* of 1826, 'its sensation was prodigious; dandies were struck dumb with envy, and washerwomen miscarried'. It was clearly an impressionable age!

Cravat knots, if perfectly tied, indicated that the wearer had time to spare, since it could take anything up to two hours to achieve the desired effect. The various types of knot had names like *populaire* ('popular'), *orientale* ('oriental'), *paresseuse* ('lazy'), *coquille de pucelle* ('niche of virginity') and *trône d'amour* ('seat of love'). Methods of cheating on

one's cravat knot began to creep into the popular guidebooks for the aspiring gentleman, as in this example from 1830:

After the knot is made take a piece of white tape and tie one end of it tight to the end of your neckcloth, then carry the tape under your arm behind your back under the other arm and fasten it tightly to the other end of your neckcloth. The tape must not be visible. This way prevents the knot from flying up.

But even this was something that could hardly be done in a hurry and it was not necessarily the key to social success. For those who did not aim so high there were paper collars, which had come on to the market by 1820, and even zinc collars, though it is hard to imagine what kind of success they could have enjoyed.

The severe, unadorned male silhouette launched by Beau Brummell remained in fashion for a hundred years. He decreed a blue woollen coat and buckskin coloured pantaloons for daywear, with immaculately polished top boots. Evening pantaloons and coats were at first either dark navy or plum, but the publication of Bulwer-Lytton's dandy novel *Pelham or the Adventures of a Gentleman* in 1828 changed all this; Pelham only ever wore black and evening dress in the main has been black ever since. *Pelham* had an enormous effect in toning down dandy fashions and dandies were even called 'pelhams' for a few years, though according to Carlisle the book itself was so dreary that he could not read to the

end, as 'magnetic sleep soon intervened'.

The sombre colours of male dress were not merely a whim of the dandy fashion leaders, for the growth of industrialization had made dark clothes a more practical proposition. The *nouveaux riches* among industrialists were beginning to gain acceptance in society and it suited them to have a costume that was sufficiently dull and anonymous to make everyone look alike. Sartorial distinction was obtained instead by precision of cut, another of Brummell's innovations, and it was in the early years of the nineteenth century that the tailors of Savile Row in London began to achieve their supremacy in tailoring – a supremacy that has lasted to the present day. At the other end of the social scale, of course, men were left with the dullness without the cut, and their clothes were as drab as their living conditions were grimy.

There were a few brighter stars, like Benjamin Disraeli, who came to one of Bulwer's parties in 'green velvet trousers, a canary coloured waistcoat, low shoes, silver buckles, lace at his wrists'. He usually wore a profusion of rings and this garb, together with the black ringlets framing his markedly Semitic features, made him so unpopular that he was not copied. Yet it was perhaps thanks to his social notoriety, expressed in his costume, that he was able to gain a foothold in politics and eventually reach the highest office. Even so he had to try five times before he was elected to Parliament.

French Dandies

As dandyism was at first a peculiarly English phenomenon the rest of Europe and America looked towards English styles and copied them. In France the whole cult was taken up with characteristic seriousness, the main link between the two countries being provided by Count Alfred d'Orsay, who carried fashions backwards and forwards.

The count exhibited true English vanity and took as much care of his looks as any woman. The British painter Benjamin Haydon (a friend of Keats) described him as wearing a 'white greatcoat, blue satin cravat, hair oiled and curling, but of the primest curve and purest water, gloves scented with eau de cologne or eau de jasmin, primrose in

Left: Lord Byron was a leader of men's fashions in a style totally opposed to Brummell's way of thinking. Where Brummell was sober, Byron was romantic. Here he is seen in an engraving after the painting by Thomas Phillips c. 1820, wearing a gold laced tartar uniform with a Turkish turban.

tint, skin in tightness'. But if anyone dared challenge the count's masculinity, he risked facing a formidable duellist. D'Orsay's brand of dandyism in fact allowed for a good deal of fantasy and variety of dress. He commonly wore six pairs of gloves a day: a pair of reindeer gloves for his morning drive; chamois for hunting; beaver for the return to Paris; kid for shopping; dogskin for a dinner party; and lambskin embroidered with silk for an evening 'rout'. Unlike Beau Brummell, however, he did not have two glovers – one to make the fingers and another to perfect the thumb. D'Orsay seemed to mature as the century advanced, settling into the sombre garments of nineteenth-century respectability.

It was the French poet Charles Baudelaire who became the philosopher of the dandies in the mid-nineteenth century. He fancied himself as a dandy and took great pains with his toilet, spending at least two hours on it even in his days of greatest poverty. His view was that dandyism can appear only in periods when democracy is not all-powerful and the aristocracy has depreciated to a certain extent; but once democracy has levelled all classes of society, dandies can no longer hold sway, since there is no room for a class whose main function is to appear decorative. Baudelaire himself wore black as a sign of mourning for increasing trade and industrial expan-

Below: Oscar Wilde in aesthetic dress in 1882, consisting of velvet jacket and knee-breeches, a silk cravat knot, and long hair.

Above left: Robespierre fancied himself as something of a dandy and is pictured, in this anonymous portrait, wearing the striped coat of revolutionary partisans in the 1790s.

Above right: By 1807 when Ingres painted this portrait of Monsieur Granet, dark romantic curls were coming into vogue and the soft folds of brown velvet added to the artistic image.

Opposite: An exotic waistcoat, loose dressing gown and turban show the perfection of leisure dress. Portrait of Comte Valotti by Vittore Ghislandi (early 19th century).

sion, which he deplored. Had he realized that he was heralding the clothes of the banker and businessman he might perhaps have modified his costume.

One innovation from France aided the dandy's attention to cleanliness. This was the discovery of the process of dry cleaning in the 1800s, the first commercial dry cleaning plant being opened in Paris by the Jolly-Bellin organization in 1845. Jean-Baptiste Jolly himself had accidentally upset an unlit lamp over his tablecloth in 1825. Impatient to get on with his work he had simply removed the cloth and did not replace it until some hours later. To his surprise, the oil-stain had completely gone, leaving this portion of the tablecloth cleaner than the rest. He immediately saw the possibilities of cleaning by spirits and was soon persuading his customers to bring back their suits for *nettoyage à sec* (dry cleaning). It was a somewhat laborious method since it involved taking the garment to pieces, dipping each section into a pan of turpentine, brushing it clean and then drying off the smell of the spirit.

Romanticism

Brummell's influence on English and

Continental fashions was firmly established by 1812, but in this year a new leader captured the imagination of London society. Lord Byron had just published *Childe Harold,* and shortly before had made his maiden speech in the House of Lords. He soon became the arbiter of a fashion entirely opposed to Brummell's, though he never intended to be anything other than an individualist and had hardly any true fashion sense at all. He would have liked to adopt dandy fashions but he suffered from two disadvantages: he was lame, and his valet was a ploughboy who would have been more at home in the fields. However, Byron managed to overcome these difficulties, choosing loose clothes that disguised his lameness and did not require much personal attention. He also loathed the constrictions of the stiff cravat and one day impatiently pulled his off, letting his high collar tumble about his throat and thus launching a new style for openneck shirts that was copied all over the world.

The romanticism of Byron's poetry and the sensual aura of his personality made him a figure of interest, so that anything he wore, however much at

variance with the general fashion, was copied by aspiring *literati*. When he returned from Albania with some handsome gold-laced Tartar uniforms and Turkish turbans, which he wore as casual dress at home, others were quick to follow suit. Byron loved exotic clothing and did not mind how garish it was. He was responsible for a flood of tasselled, embroidered velvet jackets, flowing Greek robes, upturned Turkish slippers, Ottoman dressing-gowns, Indian jewelry and strange Oriental perfumes.

The popularity of the Orient, inspired by Byron, was just beginning to ebb in the 1880s when, as we have seen, it received a fresh impetus from the publication of Sir Richard Burton's translation of the *Thousand Nights and a Night*. It was an overwhelming success, thanks probably to the growing feeling of disenchantment with England produced by the dirty factory towns and the respectable, penny-pinching outlook of the middle classes. The nineteenth-century mind was scandalized by the harem customs portrayed in the book, and an expurgated edition quickly followed, but the glamour of the East had captured people's imagination. Arthur Lazenby Liberty, who had already persuaded his employer at Farmer's and Roger's Great Cloak and Shawl Em-

Right: Edward VII loved clothes and saw himself as a leader of fashion. This photograph, taken in 1906, shows him wearing the Homburg hat which takes its name from the spa in Germany he visited as Prince of Wales.

Far right: Viscount Churchill drawn by Spy for Vanity Fair *(1904).*

porium to open an Oriental department selling Japanese prints, lacquer and porcelain, opened his own shop in Regent Street in London in 1875. He bought soft silks from Japan and had them printed in designs which recalled the East, and encouraged individual designers such as William Morris.

One of Liberty's most prominent customers, both in the clothing department and in the Oriental department, was the young Oscar Wilde, who had his own style of dress, which was adopted only by a small band of aesthetes. It consisted of knee-breeches, velvet jacket, loose flowing tie, long cape – and the inevitable green carnation in the lapel. During a lecture tour of America in 1882 he justified his attitude in a lecture with the lengthy title 'The Practical Application of the Principles of Aesthetic Theory to Exterior and Interior House Decoration, with observations upon Dress and Personal Adornments'. One of his observations was to note:

Perhaps one of the most difficult things for us to do is to choose a notable and joyous dress for men. There would be more joy in life if we were to accustom ourselves to use all the beautiful colours we can in fashioning our own clothes. The dress of the future, I think, will use drapery to a great extent and will abound in joyous colour.

Alas, how wrong he was!'

Edwardians, 'Teddy Boys' and After

On the whole dandies in the latter half of Victoria's reign tended to be a step lower down the social scale than their eighteenth- and early nineteenth-century counterparts. Their names varied as often as the fashions changed. Thus we find the 'fops' of the forties, the 'fastmen' of the late forties, the languid 'swells' of the fifties, the 'decadents' of the seventies and the 'mashers' of the eighties, to name only a few. They were all effete, had their own style of speech and were extremely 'la-di-da', as *Punch* noted.

The Edwardian age was not particularly dandified but it was a well-dressed era for men, from the fashionable creatures featured in the Spy cartoons in the magazine *Vanity Fair* to the vegetable carriers at Covent Garden, who wore a waistcoat and black necktie however shabby their condition. Edward VII himself loved dressing up and was very particular about his clothes, despite the fact that he had grown into portly middle age by the time he succeeded to the throne.

The clothes of the time were restrained and elegant. Trousers were slightly narrowed and now had turnups, jackets were a little more squared and substantial-looking at the shoulders. The shirt collar was high, with the Vs turning down at the front over a narrow black bow tie, and the top hat was the crown

Left: Edwardian dress influenced all men's wear. Even this vegetable carrier at Covent Garden Market in 1915 wears a suit with waistcoat and cravat.

Overleaf: The Melton Breakfast, engraving after a painting by Richard Dighton, showing dandies in the early 19th century, dressed for the hunt.

Above: The rock'n roll music brought fancy clothing back into men's wardrobes and this spangled suit, worn by the French singer Johnny Halliday in the sixties, followed the fifties vogue for sequins and glitter to offset body gyrations.

of respectability, giving men an important air and making them tower over their womenfolk. Dandies were people like Randolph Churchill, who had a flair for clothes, or Joseph Chamberlain, who wore a monocle, and an orchid in his buttonhole.

Then came two world wars and men's fashions were replaced by khaki. It was not until a decade after the Second World War that 'dandies' again made their appearance. The 'Teddy boys' brought in fashions that harked back to the elegance that had existed before the wars, though these styles were caricatured by young men who would never have been accepted in the Edwardian gentry class. For the Teddy boys came from the East End of London and their aim was to look not like substantial, protective father figures, but like tough guys who were to be taken note of. The padded shoulders of the jacket (called a 'drape') were accentuated, while trousers ('drainpipes') became even narrower and shoes ('winkle-pickers') had high heels and pointed toes. A 'slim Jim' tie completed the ensemble. This form of dress was not

only intended as a display of toughness to inspire male respect but had a definite element of sex appeal. The girls of the East End loved it, as the words of one from West Ham in a radio programme of 1956 show. She is describing the attire of her ideal sweetheart: 'Thick crêpe shoes. Spivvy socks. Skintight drainpipes. Stiff shirt collar. Waistcoat. Not a double-breasted coat, a one-button coat. A duffel coat and a cheese cap.'

Teddy-boy 'gear', as it became known, was not confined to the East End of London but soon spread all over the country. One Surrey county youth officer worked out statistics to show that 64 per cent of Britain's youth had had a Teddy boy or Spiv phase during their adolescence in the fifties and early sixties. Young male fashions at this time tended to change as the influence of individual pop stars or film heroes waxed and waned. Thus Marlon Brando, James Dean, Elvis Presley, Cliff Richard and the Beatles all had their day, their influence on dress being profound, if not lasting.

However, two main groups stand out in the mid-sixties – one is the Mods and

Right: A group of skinheads in 1970. The braces, striped shirts, rolled trouser legs and shaved hair styles are typical.

the Rockers, who developed the Teddy-boy fashions in two different directions. The Mods tended to adopt clean-cut Italian hairstyles and jackets, suede chukker boots and tailored trousers, and to ride scooters. The much tougher Rockers dressed for their own demi-god, the motorbike, wearing leather jackets with metal studs, zip-up boots, dirty drainpipe jeans and long greasy hair. Their successors were known as 'Hell's Angels', 'greasers' and 'bovver boys', whose clothes were similarly chosen for the violent activities they chose to engage in. Another off-shoot tough-guy fashion among youths of the early seventies, and one that is still with us at the time of writing, is that of the 'skinheads'. They wear their hair shaved very close so that they look almost bald and a feature of their dress is dungarees with coloured braces and rolled bottoms. Checks, gingham shirts and 'bovver' boots form an essential part of the outfit.

The other group which has had so much influence on fashion for the young is the 'hippies'. These originated in southern California with the 'flower people' whose philosophy of peace and love, and its corollary of 'opting out' of the middle-class desire for material wealth and possessions, filtered through to youth all over the world by means of pop groups and their music. Their new way of life and their deliberate disregard for 'smart' clothes have had a profound effect on male fashions of today.

The *raison d'être* of the dandy of the eighteenth and nineteenth centuries was to exist beautifully and to exhibit elegance and breeding as desirable aims in themselves, tinged with snobbery or the desire to achieve fame through flamboyant dress. In the twentieth century the snobbery is still there but it is of a different kind. The dandy no longer wishes to show the wealth he was born into, since this is largely irrelevant, but either to show his inherent male qualities, displayed by the virility and toughness of the skinheads etc. or by his total disregard for accepted mores and modes of dress, and this is exemplified by the pop stars of today. At the upper end of the social scale, where suavity and 'smoothness' are counted as important male attributes, virility in dress is shown less aggressively and the age-old ideals of the respectable and responsible family man are still shown in the conservativeness and sobriety of the 'city suit'. In between we have the 'Carnaby Street' image (the street in London where it all started), which has been influenced by these colourful and stylized extremes and which has led to the enormous growth in the last few years of elegant yet highly modern dress now available to all through men's boutiques. The dandy of today can afford to shop there and appear elegant and beautiful.

Above: Rupert Lycett Green helped to start Blades to cater for dandies in 1960 and remained one of the most fashionable tailors throughout the sixties. Here he is seen in a brown satin dinner suit in 1971.

Left: Hell's Angel wearing his metal-studded jacket (1969-70), an essential ingredient of the tough-guy image.

Chapter Six

American Influences

So far we have been looking at fashion largely from the English and French points of view, because they were the two countries that dominated Europe throughout the eighteenth and nineteenth centuries, with America, as long as she was politically and economically dependent on Britain, following the European lead in fashions. Now it is time to consider some of the traits peculiar to America herself and to see how it came about that American fashions are as widely copied today as their British or French counterparts were in earlier ages.

Throughout American history her people seem to have had a love–hate relationship with Britain, which prompted citizens in the New World at one time to copy British conventions slavishly, at another to defy them. For one thing the United States, even in the early days, was made up of many different races and sects, each with its own standards and manner of dress. Only in the upper echelons of society did men and women have the leisure to care about fashion, and such people were on the whole Englishmen who still had ties with the mother country. They were the provincial governors who brought their habits, in both senses, with them.

Costume in Colonial Times (1620-1776)

As far as men were concerned fashions followed the styles of France and England, though most of the early colonists rejected highly embroidered

waistcoats and fancy buttoning as inconvenient to their new state. The Puritans believed that finery was a sinful extravagance and represented wasteful expenditure of hard-earned wealth. The Dutch settlers favoured dark colours made of durable heavy woollens or leather. Even buttons 'were a vanity', as the simplest were decorative; so clothes were fastened with hooks and eyes. As prosperity increased, however, this austerity became more difficult to maintain and there was a drift towards finer dress. New settlers, who were less serious-minded than their brethren, brought cavalier modes with them, and by 1634 the Massachusetts governing body found it necessary to introduce sumptuary laws making illegal the wearing of gold or silver thread, lace, gold and silver girdles, belts or buttons, and beaver hats, and decreeing that no man or woman should make or buy slashed clothes, 'under penalty of forfeiture of such clothes'. If such articles were prohibited they must once have been worn, which seems to indicate that many of the new settlers had as great a love of finery as Europeans and that their tastes were toned down only by the weight of public opinion.

Gentlemen ordered their clothes 'blind' by simply writing to their London tailors and relatives and asking for breeches or a coat in the latest fashion. Since clothes were amply cut at this time there was no need to be over-fussy about the size. A typical order would be like this one given in a letter from Mr

Opposite: The Princess from the Land of Porcelain by *James McNeil Whistler (1864). Tales from the orient and paintings such as this inspired a vogue for eastern dress.*

Below: George Washington was a dandy in his youth and always dressed with meticulous care. This lithograph shows him in cream-coloured tight breeches and waistcoat and a military coat with epaulettes, c. 1780s.

Fitz-John Winthrop to his brother in 1706: 'I desire you to bring me a very good camlet cloak lyned with what you like except blew. It may be purple or red or striped with those other colours if so worn suitable and fashionable.... I would make a hard shift rather than not have the cloak.' This gentleman wrote so many letters in this vein to his brother that the latter was finally induced to write suggesting that he should wear out the clothes he had before ordering anything new. But requests continued and it is interesting to see from their correspondence that, careless as he was about the exact colour or cut of his coats, he was extremely particular about details such as buttonholes, sending repeated requests for drawings of the latest style.

Another connoisseur who was concerned about minute details was Governor Jonathan Belcher, whose portrait shows that he had buttonholes on his cuffs embroidered in the shape of curled ostrich plumes, the end of the plume being formed by a little tassel of fringed silk. This gentleman was a typical colonial figure, a union of the New Englander and the English courtier. His wealth, acquired by inheritance and a keen interest in mercantile life, fitted him for a position of responsibility, and he was governor of Massachusetts from 1730 to 1741. His position also demanded that his appearance should impress people, so he too wrote to England stating his requirements. This letter is dated 1773:

I have desired my brother Mr Partridge, to get me some cloaths made, and that you should make them and have sent him the yellow gogram suit you made me at London; but those you make now must be 2 or 3 inches longer and as much bigger. Let 'em be workt strong, as well as neate and curious. I believe Mr Hants in Spittlefields (of whom I had the last) will let you have the gogram as cheap as anybody.

Gogram was a mixture of silk and mohair. With this suit he ordered 'a very handsome sword knot, cane string and cockade all of orange ribbon richly flowered with silver and crimson'.

Colonists such as Governor Belcher believed that dress 'had a moral effect upon the conduct of mankind'; it was a badge of rank. Thus class distinctions in clothes did operate in America, though mainly in the towns and at country meetings in the north. Southerners appreciated the importance of an impressive appearance in their own way. Wigs in particular were felt to add distinction, even to house servants, who were obliged to wear them whenever it was necessary to enhance their

Below: Portrait of an unknown American settler in 1720 in an outfit obviously ordered from England. Fancy buttonholes, like these, were favoured by those who could afford them.

Below right: The turban and banyan (a loose-flowing, brocaded robe) was popular for leisure wear especially in America where the climate discouraged tightly fitting garments. Nicholas Boylston chose to have his portrait painted by John Singleton Copeley in this garb in 1767.

Left: Patchwork of printed cotton in the traditional 'pineapple' pattern, made in the United States in the second half of the nineteenth century.

Below: A present-day model wears an olive green quilted bonnet and pelisse featuring the high waisted empire line, c. 1815.

master's status. Even rogues and vagabonds who had been deported to America were supplied with second-hand wigs, so that they had a chance of cutting a respectable figure and obtaining a position such as that of schoolmaster. But on the whole southern planters, perhaps because they lived in a hotter region, went about their daily affairs more carelessly dressed than their northern counterparts. The *London Magazine* remarked on this fact in 1745:

Tis an odd sight that except some of the very elevated Sort few Persons wear Perukes; so that, you would imagine they were all sick or going to bed; common people wear Woolen and Yarn caps, but the better ones wear White Holland or Cotton. Thus they travel 50 miles from Home. It may be cooler for aught I know, but methinks 'tis very ridiculous.

Probably the garb described was similar to the turban and banyan worn by English countrymen in their own homes.

Southern ladies found it harder to keep up with the fashions than northerners, who could go down to the wharves when foreign ships came in and choose lengths of Indian gauzes and muslins, Italian silks and Dutch linens to make up into their own gowns. Southern ladies had to send lists of their requirements to London merchants, who would be paid with the proceeds of the next tobacco crop. Then they waited patiently for ships to bring them year-old fashions. One London house had thirty Virginia planters to whom it sent an annual supply of apparel, either partly made up or in lengths. The women were very much at the mercy of the merchant, for there were few or no fashion plates or magazines in colonial days for them to choose from. The best they could hope for was to go to Charleston or Annapolis – centres of elegance in the South – and somehow or other contrive to get hold of the latest fashions, or at least obtain ideas on how to make up or trim a gown. These ladies followed the lead of Paris, as interpreted by London, as

101

Above: A lady with a parasol and veiled hat visits a friend at home; painting by William Merritt Chase (1896). Both ladies wear dresses with exaggerated sleeves, which served the purpose of narrowing the waist.

closely as possible, the only marked difference being that gowns were a little looser in the sleeve and a few inches shorter at the hem, because of the heat.

The heat was also responsible for a fashion that was hardly known in England, for though England dictated a white complexion as the ideal of beauty, there was little direction as to how this could be preserved in a hot country. So Americans wore sun-expelling masks held on long sticks, rather like ladies at a masked ball. Even children had to wear them, as we know from George

Washington's order for masks for his stepchildren. Riding masks were fitted with a silver mouthpiece, which the lady could keep between her teeth to leave her hands free.

Indigenous Influences

In eighteenth-century society fashion was the privilege of the moneyed few: the masses wore cast-offs or reach-me-downs and odd combinations of clothes bought second-hand. Those who had new clothes made would order approximations of the garments they saw around them, if indeed they lived in areas where people were fashionably dressed. But the early Americans were pioneers, many of whom struck away from the cities and founded their own homesteads and shanty towns. They had to rely on themselves for their clothes and they had very little time or energy to spare for following complicated cut and style. By the mid-nineteenth century however patchwork quilts and coats were being made, which were the fruit of any spare moments the housewife enjoyed. Though patchwork originated in Great Britain it achieved its true flowering in America, where it was seen as an economy and an opportunity to make an artistic and useful artifact, made as it was from scraps of old clothes or bits of fabric sewn together in a variety of traditional patterns. Some of these involved religious motifs such as the Star of David; others were inspired by political events, like the 'Radical Rose' of the nineteenth century, with its

black patches symbolizing the growing Negro problem. Others were simply geometrical designs, though much more complex than the honeycomb pattern that needlewomen adopt today. They showed distinct traces of Red Indian influences, for the Indian method of ornamenting hides and working dyed porcupine quills entailed similar geometric problems. Though the poetic meaning of such designs was not understood, the early settlers did not disdain to borrow them. It is interesting to note here that patchwork has periodically had repercussions in the world of fashion, the latest being the machine-made patchwork skirts, coats and jackets of the first years of the 1970s.

The Red Indian influence on American clothes from the eighteenth to the twentieth century is very marked. The soft skin slippers and footwear worn for sport by contemporary Americans derive directly from the Indian moccasin. Also Red Indian is the tradition for

Below: A lively painting in the style of the American primitives, third quarter of the nineteenth century, depicts a quilting party, a common occasion of American country life. When all the patches for the traditional quilt had been sewn, friends and neighbours were called in to help with the final assembly.

Above: Elias Howe's sewing machine, patented in the United States in 1846.

Below: A portrait of Mrs Samuel Chandler by Winthrop Chandler, 1780, showing a costume which follows Parisian trends, but with distinctly American severity. Mrs Chandler wears a mob cap with lapets.

finishing off leather jackets and bags by cutting long fringes into the edge, a detail that has been popular at various periods. Pearl Binder in *The Peacock's Tail* (1958) even traces the tight American trouser seat to the Redskin dislike of having the buttocks covered. Their own leg covering had no seat at all, so the first thing they did when they received trousers from the Palefaces was to cut out the seat. The white colonist dared not copy this feature, but a part of him perhaps envied the frank display of male virility and he tightened the seat on his own trousers accordingly. Duffel coats, too, have connections with the Indians. Though the fabric originated in the town of Duffel in Flanders, it was later made in England for winter wear in America. The thick, tufted, knotted nap was unpopular among the citizens of the United States and coats made up in duffel were therefore sold off to the Red Indians. Later, when weaving techniques had rectified their coarseness, they were reinstated and unleashed a fashion rage that has lasted in Europe until the present day.

Foreign Contacts

With the Declaration of Independence in Philadelphia in 1776 patriotic Americans cut their ties with Britain, transferring their allegiance, as far as clothes were concerned, to France. In fact as British and French fashions influenced each other, their dress differed only slightly from that of the British. There were differences, of course, for the Americans wore revolutionary cockades in their hats and buttons bearing Washington's portrait or the patriotic basket, but all in all costume in revolutionary times was no less fine than in the old land. The Chevalier de Crèvecoeur noted, 'If there is a town on the American continent where English luxury displayed all its follies it is in New York . . . . In the dress of women you will see the most brilliant silks, gauzes, hats and borrowed hair.' Some, like John Adams's wife, who accompanied her husband to England in 1784 when he became first minister, even thought the English more dowdy:

I am not a little surprised to find dress, unless on public occasions, so little regarded here. The gentlemen are very plainly dressed, the ladies much less so than with us. Tis true you must put a hoop on and have your hair dressed, but a common straw hat, no cap, with only a ribbon on the crown is thought sufficient dress to go into company.

Meanwhile Benjamin Franklin's popularity in Paris led to everything American becoming the vogue in France. In terms of fashion this probably meant merely that the popularity of the straw hat, originally an American fashion and popular country wear in England and Europe, was assured.

Far more important adjustments had to be made when America was cut off from Europe by the Napoleonic Wars, for the country was thrown back on her own resources. Women could not obtain French silks or English wools, so instead they took to wearing cottons and calicoes and chintzes. Calico was the strongest of the three and could be printed in many fanciful designs such as 'liberty peak', 'basketwork', 'Ranelagh half

Left: During the Napoleanic wars, the States were cut off from French silks and English wools and were forced to fall back on their own chintzes and calicoes, which had been associated with country wear. The engraving shows calicoes being printed with traditional designs.

moon' or 'harlequin moth'. Some calicoes even had portraits of Franklin and Washington stamped on them.

Patriotism was rife at this period and Presidents Thomas Jefferson and James Monroe were working towards a policy of opposition to outside interference in the Americas (finally made explicit in the 'Monroe Doctrine' of 1823) that was to terminate only with the sinking of the United States ship *Lusitania* during the First World War. But in the more frivolous world of fashion women were quietly taking as little notice as they could without completely abandoning patriotism. One innovation, the publication of fashion magazines, helped them in this, for they could genuinely sponsor American industries while still culling their ideas from European sources of fashion. The *Ladies' European Magazine*, first published in London in 1798, was one of the first to cross the Atlantic, followed in 1806 by the more popular journal *La Belle Assemblée*, which changed its name to the *Court Magazine & Belle Assemblée* in 1832. It now contained a letter from Paris specially designed to keep all those who did not live in that city in touch with the court of the 'Great Mogul', as Horace Walpole called fashion. The first American newspaper to print a regular dress column seems to have been *Port Folio*, a Philadelphia paper published between 1861 and 1865, while America was cut off from European influences during the Civil War.

During these years of strife Southern belles kept abreast of fashion if they could. Opportunists broke though the blockades bringing silks, petticoat hoops and accessories to the girls who were willing to pay high prices for them. The alternative was to stuff their shoes with newspapers to keep out the wind and to line their dresses with old rags to keep them warm. Ladies even wore gaiters made of old shawls or cut-up carpets in the colder seasons and many may, like Scarlett O'Hara in *Gone With the Wind*, have cut up the curtains to make a new gown for an important occasion. Thus Rhett Butler is an important figure in the minds of the Atlanta ladies, especially when he is able to bring one of them the otherwise unobtainable white satin for her wedding dress and also give her hints on how it should be made up to match the latest Paris styles. Margaret Mitchell writes:

'Had he been less obviously masculine, his ability to recall details of dresses, bonnets and coiffures would have been put down as the rankest effeminacy. The ladies always felt a little odd when they besieged him with questions about styles, but they did it nevertheless. They were isolated from the world of fashion as shipwrecked mariners, for few books of fashion came through the blockade. For all they knew the ladies of France might be shaving their heads and wearing coonskin caps . . . .'

Then, during the difficult years of the reconstruction, the old cotton-planting

Below: Elizabeth Fry in 1820 wearing Quaker clothing. The shawl was an essential part of the costume and her bonnet later became known as 'The Fry'.

aristocracy were too poor to follow fashions and could only glower at the Yankee ladies or the carpet-baggers and scallawags who sported the narrower hoops and shorter jackets that Paris was now wearing. It was a difficult time for the South and it was a decade before the old guard had adapted to new ways of life and fashions in the re-united States and returned to their system of following French and English influences. There were, of course, movements such as the mid-century Rational Dress Campaign (see page 49), which sought to establish clothing suitable to the American way of life, but it was not until later in the century that the idea gained any real influence.

Quaker Dress

Most of the Quakers who emigrated to the New World settled in Pennsylvania, where William Penn had formed a strong Quaker community. Their sober ideas were expressed in the solemnity of their dress, which tended towards greys and browns, with shawls and bonnets for the women and the obligatory hat for gentlemen. This hat was something of a bone of contention, since for many years the Quakers could not agree among themselves on whether it was right to have the head covered on all occasions, including social engagements and before God, or whether on these two occasions the head-dress might be omitted. Extremist Quakers were adamant that hats must always be worn, and Penn himself had to bail out two cousins of his in England who were committed to Newgate Prison for no greater crime than refusing to take off their chimney-pot hats when giving evidence during a trial. Hat-wearers also risked ostracism from non-Quaker members of the community, not so much because they advertised their religion as because it was thought that they showed social disrespect by appearing with their heads covered. Joseph John Gurney, the brother of the English Quakeress Elizabeth Fry, describes his appearance at a dinner party in 1810:

'For three weeks before I was in agitation from the knowledge that I must enter the drawing room with my hat on. From this sacrifice, strange and unaccountable as it

may seem, I could not escape. In a Friend's attire and with my hat on I entered the drawing room at the dreaded moment, shook hands with the mistress of the house, went back into the hall, deposited my hat and returned home in some degree of peace . . . . I was asked no more.'

This was at the time when all the fashionable world wore Empire gowns and Quaker ladies' gowns were correspondingly shorter waisted. Similarly, when leg-of-mutton sleeves appeared Quaker sleeves swelled out, while with the appearance of hoops their skirts grew wider.

Quaker fashions in fact had their origins in Paris, though they were more modestly interpreted; or at least their leaders hoped that this was so and spoke sternly against those who let their heads

Above: An American primitive painting by an unknown artist 1825-30 of a Mrs Seth Wilkinson. The painting shows careful attention to the details of dress. The lap dog is seen as an accessory to the costume.

Opposite: 'Sunday Morning in front of a Quaker Meeting House'; water colour by Pavel Petrovich Svinin (1804). Both sexes are dressed in sober greys and browns and even the child is forced to wear a hat. The ladies are wearing the calash bonnet.

be turned by such frivolities. As early as 1726 Hannah Hill delivered a speech to a meeting of women Friends railing against hoops and gowns with superfluous folds at the back and telling them that they should not wear striped stockings or carry fans, 'lest it direct the mind from the more inward and spiritual exercises which all ought to be concerned in. And also that Friends do not accustom themselves to go with bare breasts or bare necks.'

A good Friend was expected to wear a clean white apron over her gown and a bonnet to cover her hair. The calash, a bonnet resembling a pram or baby-carriage hood, was a popular form of head covering. It originated in the late eighteenth century, and as it developed the arrangement of folds and plaits became the distinguishing mark of a Hicksite from a Gurneyite or a Gurneyite from a Wilburite. The most common bonnet was Elizabeth Fry's 'coal-scuttle' or 'sugar-scoop' bonnet. A shawl was worn to complete the ensemble, in spite of the fact that *La Belle Assemblée* declared that 'it turns any female NOT beautiful and elegant into an absolute DOWDY'. One imagines that the costume of Quakeresses was indeed dowdy, but

it was intentionally so, for the aim was to look neat and clean, not elegant and startling; indeed their main influence on fashion lay in extending this concept of cleanliness to others in less privileged positions. One of Elizabeth Fry's greatest achievements when she began to visit Newgate Prison in 1814 was to teach the women inmates self-respect and respect for their appearance. She was so successful that they would even sit docilely sewing while she read them Bible stories. It was the aim of every American Quakeress to extend her influence in this way.

Functional Dress

The pioneers in the mid-West have probably been responsible for America's major contributions to modern fashion. The bright plaid lumbershirt that the all-American kid now wears derives from a specific function: its glowing pattern was dictated by the need for the lumberjack to be clearly visible to his mates among the dangers that beset him from tree-felling in the gloomy forests or from the turbulent currents of the unfreezing rivers. Similarly, dungarees originated as the unpretentious dress of the worker in the gold mines. The cut

Below: Gold miners wearing the denim jeans made by Levi-Strauss in 1882. The rivets, which are still a feature of 'levis' were added as reinforcements to stop the weight of the gold nuggets tearing the pockets.

Below right: An advertisement for the popular miners' jeans made by Levi-Strauss, 1882. The spring bottoms, or flares, were designed to fit over boots.

Left: Croquet, American-style, satirized by Punch *in 1864. The women are dressed in the bloomer costume. The exaggerated size of the hoops and clubs indicates the British belief that everything in America was bigger and better than in England.*

Below: Gold satin evening dress by the American designer Charles James, 1934. It has a low neckline, shoulder straps and is bias-cut to emphasize the figure. The bias-cut was invented by Mme Vionnet.

was roomy and the numerous pockets were strategically placed for easy access to tools. Dungarees have travelled a stage further in recent times to become a fancy-dress garment for daring girls with good figures. All the pockets are still there, but purely for decoration. Only the car mechanic and plumber now put this garment to its proper purpose. When he lectured in New York after touring the United States, Oscar Wilde told his fashionable audience that the only well-dressed men he had seen were the miners in the West, for he believed that whatever is truly fit for its purpose is beautiful in its own manner:

'Their well brimmed hats which shaded them from the sun and protected them from the rain, and the cloak which is by far the most beautiful piece of drapery ever invented, may well be dwelt on with admiration.

The high boots too were sensible and practical. They wore only what was comfortable and therefore beautiful.'

Another garment designed purely for function and durability was the pair of blue 'levis' designed by Levi-Strauss for the gold-rush miners in 1850. The original trousers were made of tent material, which Levi-Strauss had brought with him when he emigrated from Bavaria, but their success was soon so well established that he started making them in more comfortable heavyweight den-

im. An indigo dye was used, as it was cheap, and in the late 1860s copper rivets were added to give extra strength. Levi jeans became regulation wear for cowboys, railroaders, lumberjacks, oil drillers and other labourers. Now they are fashion wear and show hardly any change from 120 years ago, except that they have become slightly more tight-fitting and are available in many colours. Until 1968 girls who were attracted to levi trousers had to buy men's, but they are now being made with female shapes in mind.

The blue jeans were taken up by the younger generation in the West, who found their durability suitable to the active lives they led. The jeans and fancy blouses worn by Los Angeles girls in 1945 became the prototypes of the separates that achieved growing popularity in the next generation. The impetus for garments such as T-shirts, playsuits, trousers and shorts also came from America. They represent the antithesis of the sheltered lady's existence and are the ultimate expression of the cult of youth.

American Couture

Youthfulness was also expressed in the clothes created by young American designers when the country was cut off from European influences during the world wars. The first all-American fashion show was held in New York in

1914, its success ensured by the sponsorship of *Vogue*, which had first come out in the United States in 1892 and at that time was edited by Edna Woolman Chase. She had a genius for picking out clothes that would appeal to the youth of America, but she was not, on that account, biased in favour of American designers. Throughout the postwar period she selected clothes shown at couture houses in Paris, London and New York strictly on the basis of merit and gave them coverage and credit in the pages of *Vogue*, which was the first magazine to give both the name of the original couture house and the name of the shop where copies of the model could be bought. Its date of publication was timed each season to coincide with the arrival of the new clothes in the shops. *Vogue* offices opened in Paris and London, the only other magazine to follow suit being *Harper's Bazaar*. But neither of these magazines could compete with the authoritative fashion reports in the strictly non-glossy publication *Women's Wear Daily*, founded in New York in 1910. This paper, which is still to be found in

Left: Antonio Donghi: La cocottina *(1925). The simple, ageless shoes and dress could almost be modern.*

Opposite: Pablo Picasso's Portrait of Olga in an armchair *is dated 1917, and shows the bare arms and neck which became the hallmark of the twenties.*

111

*Above: Jean Harlow in a
white sequined negligée in a
pose typical of the Hollywood
film star of the 1930s.*

spiration from workaday garb and also from Mexican peasant costumes. In the forties the summer was made gayer by their pretty dresses with frills and flounces.

Probably the most influential American fashion designer (and certainly prophet in his own times) was Rudi Gernreich, who launched the topless dress in the early sixties and has lived to see his style of undress taken up in the seventies on the beaches of St Tropez.

American designers were aided too by the development of new fibres and fabrics that originated in their research laboratories. The discovery of nylon has already been mentioned and other synthetic fibres soon followed. The new fabrics were not at first favoured by designers because they tended to be coarse and shiny, but as techniques improved an interchange between fabric manufacturer and designer grew up, so that designers are now expected to view some 60 to 200 new samples each year before they begin working on their collections.

The Hollywood Influence

No survey of American fashions would be complete without a mention of Hollywood stars like Jayne Mansfield and Marilyn Monroe, who created new styles of sex appeal in dress, with garments fitting closely over the hips and featuring a new centre of fashion interest – the bust cleavage. Bras changed their shape and padding came into vogue, to give every girl the feeling that she could have, as French advertisements put it, 'la véritable busty-look New Yorkaise'. Glamour and wealth were expressed in the mink coat worn by every famous film actress in the fifties and coveted by every society lady. The general desire for furs was satisfied in the next decade when cheaper skins became fashionable. From 1968 even an office girl could afford to treat herself to what became known as a 'fun fur', which made her feel as glamorous as her richest contemporaries.

The Drab American Male

The view that America is a predominantly matriarchal society receives some confirmation in the corresponding drabness of male attire. Apart from the in-

every fashion house, gives reports on every single collection in every capital and has features on fashion personnel all over the world.

During the Second World War American designers began to make a name for themselves. Hattie Carnegie, Bonnie Cashin, Claire McCardle, Claire Potter, Tom Brigance, Charles James, Norman Norell and Howard Greer were the names best known to the American shopper. Then after the blockade of Paris America's best couturier, Mainbocher, returned to his native land after many years' absence in the capital of fashion to set up a fashion house in New York. His great experience, combined with his own individual flair, inspired the designers round him and thus raised the standard of American couture. The chic uniforms he designed for servicewomen have already been mentioned. He also encouraged designers to look to their own heritage rather than try to follow trends abroad; under his influence they looked towards the youthful fashions of the mid-West, gaining innovation of the soft shirt in the early twentieth century and the coloured shirts and wider neckties of the twenties, the predominant male fashion has remained the traditional business suit, however unsuited to the extremes of the American climate. One American dress-designer, Elizabeth Hawes, thinks that this dull business dress illustrates the timidity of the male, which she blames on American puritanism:

'Puritanically they deny themselves their rights to the pursuit of all the mental and physical satisfaction women can get from dressing . . . . What a lot of snobbery there is in our democracy. Is it a sign of the aristocracy we aren't supposed to have here to wear four thicknesses of material about the neck?'

Innovations such as Hawaiian flowered shirts flourish today in some city offices but depend on the kudos attached to the job: the aspiring banker prefers to appear in strictly formalized wear, whereas the budding film director, television floor manager or pop singer experience few inhibitions and even find that unconventional clothes enhance their image. Experiments to initiate more comfortable 'uniforms' have been tried. The bank clerks of the Tompkins County Trust Company in Central New York State, for example, were all clapped into Bermuda shorts for the summer of 1955. Ageing, pot-bellied businessmen appeared in black, white or plaid shorts and bright, youthful knee socks, still smoking the fraternal cigar and apparently quite at their ease since they were all dressed alike. In 1956 the doormen at the Raleigh Hotel in Washington were persuaded to wear a similar costume, to the secret chagrin of the elderly commissionaire, who was observed surreptitiously trying to pull his socks up over his ageing knees. Such dress is certainly utilitarian but it is doubtful whether it will be universally adopted even in hot countries. At least the anonymous city suit, depressing though it is, has the convenience of ironing out differences in age and class and avoids the embarrassment of older men donning unsuitable garments intended solely for the young and fair.

Above: A publicity picture of Marilyn Monroe at the preview of The Seven Year Itch *(1955) emphasizing her sex-appeal image.*

Chapter Seven

Postscript Couture and After

Fashion in the last decade has seen the rise of youth culture mirrored in the upward climb of the miniskirt. Clothing has been so closely identified with broader sociological movements that the 'permissive society' actually meant the see-through blouse, the thigh-high skirt and uninhibited, extravert clothing, as well as the morals and mores of the wearers.

In the 1970s fashion has steadied down from the wildest extravagances of the so-called 'swinging sixties'. The higher cost of materials and labour, plus a natural swing reaction, have combined to encourage a return to a more classic way of dressing. But the landscape now looks entirely different from 10 years ago. Internationally known couturiers have died – or shut the gilded doors of their establishments. Increasingly, fashion goliaths among department stores and manufacturers have been decimated by the assault of youthful designers and young-style shops. Above all, the idea of fashion dictatorship – by designers, by buyers, by fashion editors, or simply by ladies of taste and discrimination – has been universally abandoned. Ever since the march past of miniskirts and boots, fashions in clothing, jewelry and even hairstyles have been dictated from the street. The attempt to bring hemlines down with the midi, or calf-length skirt, was the last and final attempt to bring the recalcitrant modern woman to heel. Its failure cost hundreds of manufacturers in Europe and America their livelihood and ended the traditional dominance of Paris couture.

Because the movement away from positive fashion directives coincided with the rise of Women's Liberation and general feminist militancy, the current anarchy is partly sociological. The refusal of intelligent women to be used as pawns of the rag trade or to be exploited as sex objects for men is laudable and sincere. But for every woman who enjoys 'doing her own thing', there are many others who feel bewildered or bemused by choice. The chances of women permanently refusing *en masse* to be fashion's slaves therefore seem remote.

The last 15 years of fashion can be roughly divided into three parts: the rise of the upstarts (Mary Quant, the boutique boom, the youth cult); the capitulation of the giants (Paris couture turning commercial, the stores launching their own boutiques); anarchy (the hippies, psychedelia, flower power, Victoriana, Indiana and flea-market clothes).

The Technical Revolution

Scattered among these broad movements that have spanned the last decade are the technological advances that made many of the fashions possible. It has often been said that without the invention of the zip the fashion history of the twentieth century would have had to be rewritten. The miniskirt could not have risen so high without the mass production of cheap stocking tights. Topless fashions could not have become reality without

Opposite: This afternoon dress drawn by Georges Barbier in 1912 shows that some women in France were attempting to break away from the tightly corsetted figures of the previous decade, though it was not until the war that the tyranny was finally broken.

Below: French midinettes (the actual seamstresses) on strike in Paris, 1923.

Mme IDA RUBINSTEIN
Créatrice de "La Pisanelle"
Habillée par Worth

Above: 'Coco' Chanel photographed by Cecil Beaton in 1936 wearing a simple dinner-gown of her own creation. The string of pearls round her neck was the hallmark of her designs.

Above right: Ida Rubenstein wearing a dress designed by Worth for her appearance in La Pisanelle (1913).

Far right: Every year Dior gave a new name to the silhouette he featured in his collections. In 1954-5 three letters of the alphabet were used to express the dominant shapes, seen here from left to right, A, S, and H.

the no-bra bras – sheer clinging cups of stretch nylon that altered all the accepted ideas of underwear. Stretch vinyl brought the knee-high boot to the calves first of teenagers, and then of the whole female population. The widespread use of man-made fibres has done more than any fashion to break down class distinctions in dress – and to free women from the drudgery of hand washing and ironing. Ironically enough, the ecological movement that has encouraged a return to natural 'peasant' fibres such as raw cotton and calico has been purely a high fashion, accepted by those rich enough to cope with the problems of maintenance, or young enough not to care. Crimplene, Terylene, Lycra (and their international equivalents) are the names that most often appear on the vast mass of clothing labels.

The Giants and the Giant Killers

But inevitably, it is the organization of the industry that seems to have undergone the most cataclysmic changes of our time – in particular the decline in influence and prestige of Paris haute couture. The fact that the high fashion collections survived the wartime break,

and all the subsequent problems of labour and production, was due chiefly to the French government. They subsidized (and still do) the couture industry, as a showcase for French design in clothing. The upsurge of enthusiasm in the post-war period was the result of the dazzling brilliance of individual designers, notably Christian Dior with his New Look and Cristobal Balenciaga with the Sack.

In 1963, when Mary Quant's name first became a household word in Britain, Paris designers were still a tightly knit group organized under the guidance of the Chambre Syndicale de la Couture Parisienne, their trade union. Invitations were rigidly limited, showings dramatic and secret, tendency sketches and photographs permitted only with express authorization – and mostly a month or so later to avoid copyists. But the larger houses such as Dior and Balmain had already faced up to the fact that the money was coming from the United States rather than Europe, and from perfume and accessories rather than made-to-measure clothing. By the end of the sixties this was to lead to an ever-increasing dissemination of couture names on anything from chocolates (Pierre Cardin) to sunglasses (Dior) to bath towels (Saint Laurent). The acceptance of a commercial key to success was also to spawn off-the-peg designer collections, and meant the final triumph of ready-to-wear over haute couture.

But for the moment the couturiers were still considered as a laboratory of ideas. The only trouble was that some of the best and most influential ideas did not stem from them, or even from France.

Swinging London

Mary Quant had actually set up her first 'Bazaar' shop in the King's Road, Chelsea, in London, with her husband Alexander Plunket Greene as early as 1955, when they both left art school. In 1963 she founded a wholesale operation called the Ginger Group, which was to spread the name of Quant and the offbeat style she represented across the world. The clothes at that stage were a rebellion against the tight skirts and formal suits that made a girl who came of the age to wear them instantly a

'woman'. The word 'teenager' might have been invented solely for the gym-slip dresses, the stripy stockings, the casual coats and short skirts that Mary Quant produced. Her message reverberated – into three shops of her own, into a mushroom growth of boutiques and ultimately into a reappraisal of retailing methods by the staid stores. What Quant did for women's clothes and the King's Road, Chelsea, her compatriot John Stephen did for men and Carnaby Street – a narrow alley between Soho and Regent Street in the West End of London. Both places are now internationally honoured as monuments to the youth cult they epitomized.

Couture and Ready-to-Wear

But while Mary Quant and the Beatles were giving birth to 'Swinging London' (a phrase actually coined by *Time Magazine* in the United States), a saviour appeared in Paris, in a stark white salon in traditional couture land. André Courrèges, a Basque-born fashion designer, brought the miniskirt to flower in French soil – and allowed the French to claim it as their own. His crisp, geometrically cut dresses and trouser.suits, sculpted from thick white wool gaberdine by a man who wore tennis shoes and a T-shirt, started a fashion revolution that still had its repercussions 10 years later. His flat white boots, so necessary to the short-skirted silhouette, appeared in main streets in Chicago, Tokyo and London. Courrèges, like so

many fashion prophets, found himself with much honour but no money, since his ideas were mercilessly plagiarized. He shut his salon in fury in 1965, reopening 18 months later with his own ready-to-wear range, which was widely exported. His move set a pattern for the future of French haute couture.

Other Paris designers were internationally admired during the sixties. Pierre Cardin's space-age fashions and incredibly ingenious cut became hallmarks of the decade. Yves Saint Laurent, a shy bespectacled young man who was trained at the House of Dior and set up under his own name in 1961, was to influence women with his severe black tunic and trousers, and shock them with his transparent blouse. He remains the only Paris couturier of any real international importance and fashion stature, although in 1971 he gave up haute couture showings except to a small group of private clients, and now markets his image via his Rive Gauche ready-to-wear shops. In the long term the association of haute couture with gimmicks such as unisex, see-through blouses and hot pants was to lead to its downfall. In the middle sixties fashion was literally the most fashionable subject around. What Beatle wives (to say nothing of Jackie Kennedy) wore to film premières and airport departures became front-page news. Paris couturiers came in for an explosion of publicity, which they were unable to sustain. Even if the creative inspiration had been

Above left: Christian Dior at work creating a new evening gown, draping the fabric over the model. Dior would do hundreds of sketches before settling on his theme for a collection.

Above centre: A Dior (London) outfit for 1970 designed by Jorn Langberg showing a suede cape edged with matching fox fur worn over culottes and an embroidered waistcoat. The fox fur hat and velvet boots complete the outfit.

Above right: Two winter outfits for the Dior collection, 1972.

Art - Goût - Beauté

*Left: An evening ensemble in
red velvet trimmed with fur
and embroidery formed part
of Poiret's collection for 1922.*

*Above: Vendeuses cope with
ladies who have come to order
their clothes from the House
of Paquin in 1907.*

there, the process of evolution and
gestation (and, of course, the cost) of
couture was totally unsuited to the
instant obsolescence of throw-away
fashion movements. The momentum
died, and rising stars on the ready-to-
wear scene soon outshone the once great
names of Paris.

Again, it was the French government
that took the lead in redirecting their
fashion impetus, by encouraging a Salon
du Prêt-à-Porter, or Ready-to-Wear Fair,
which by 1970 had grown into a gigantic
export industry and taken over a huge
plate-glass exhibition hall at the Porte
de Versailles in Paris, which had been
purpose built for such export fairs.
While the haute couture people sniffed
out a new market in couture-branded
perfumes – they had cornered two-
thirds of the world's perfume sales by
1971 – ready-to-wear designers like
Jean Cacharel, Daniel Hechter and Em-

manuelle Khanh became France's new
prestige names. Most of the couturiers
still show high-fashion collections in
January and July, but these are pre-
empted by their own ready-to-wear collections, shown alongside the biannual
salons three months previously.

International Markets

Great Britain instigated its own export
fashion fairs in 1967, under the auspices
of the Clothing Export Council of Great
Britain, who are also active in arranging
British promotions overseas. The Ger-
mans have tended to dominate Europe
at their fabric and mass-production
fairs. The Italians (and to a much lesser
extent the Spaniards) have managed to
carve themselves an export fashion
market in precisely the areas of glamour
and luxury that the French have partly
abandoned.

118

*Right: A coat
and muff by
Patou (1929),
emphasizing a
lengthening of the
line.*

Above: An evening gown by Balmain (1954) taken against a photographer's backdrop – a typical accompaniment to fashion photography of the period.

Above centre: Hubert de Givenchy followed Dior's lead in 1955 with an A-line inspired dress made of grey wool with a pouched jacket.

Above right: Nina Ricci's clothes were known for their feminity and luxuriousness. This ample coat (1962) combines the convenience of a coat with the flamboyance of a cape.

The commercial exploitation of famous Paris names has frequently been undertaken by American companies. Beauty firms in particular have been willing to back loss-making high-fashion showings in return for worldwide publicity, and the right to market a couture perfume. This, coupled with the American store buyers' enthusiasm for couture toiles (a cotton blueprint of a design) made the United States the most revered consumer and promoter of haute couture during the 1960s.

Perhaps the most surprising fashion star to rise in the seventies has been that of Japan. Her economic growth has resulted in a flood of Japanese buyers in the European market-place. One of Paris's most important ready-to-wear designers, especially for knitwear, is Kenzo Takaya, one of several ex-patriate Japanese who have managed to challenge France's most jealously guarded skill. A Japanese decision to buy up all available stocks of Australian wool has pushed up prices alarmingly in Europe and North America and put the Japanese in the influential commercial position once reserved for customers from the United States.

In all major fashion capitals clothing is now divided into a small number of designer collections, and many wholesale fashion houses who mass-produce basic lines. The American industry is far more streamlined and efficient than most of its European counterparts, but all work on the same principle of wide dissemination of an original inspiration. The way in which snakeskin moved from being a high-fashion leather to a mass-market print in the three years between 1967 and 1970 is a good example of this. In spite of inflation, fashion is probably now available more widely and at more reasonable prices than ever before. But fashion in the real sense of the word is chiefly a youth movement, as spare money for clothing ephemera is naturally the prerogative of those who have few commitments for their wages.

Right: Jacqueline Onassis (formerly Kennedy) in 1971.

The Main Trends

What are the fashion movements that will in retrospect stand out in recent times? Inevitably, the rise and fall of the miniskirt has dominated the last decade. It started an ever-growing trend towards sportswear and away from formal wear that has greatly influenced both men's and women's clothing. As we have seen, the male as a peacock is not a new phenomenon in fashion history, but it was certainly a distinguishing mark of the sixties. Men today are probably more fashion conscious (and that includes cosmetic products such as after-shaves and deodorants) than at any time in the twentieth century. But in spite of Women's Lib it is still women's clothes, and the various ways in which they reveal or conceal their forms, that capture the imagination and the headlines.

The unisex movement of the early sixties led to an acceptance of the trouser suit for women and the almost universal wearing of trousers by women in their everyday life. Casual pleated skirts, separates and knitted sweaters have been the kingpin of female wardrobes ever since Chanel made them fashionable, and at the moment there seems

Left: Yves Saint Laurent was the first couturier to break completely with the Paris traditions, cutting off his association with the Chambre Syndicate and producing a range of off-the-peg styles for all age groups. This pleated midi-skirt is from his 1971 collection.

Below left: A Mary Quant ensemble for 1972, featuring a tie-bow top and pants cut away to reveal the navel.

Below centre: Mary Quant's early successes were with little girl gymslip dresses, a theme that was still apparent in this child-like dress for 1972.

Below right: A cotton gingham maxi-skirt with matching coloured large-check jacket from Mary Quant's 1973 collection.

Opposite: Kees Van Dongen:
The Marchesa Casati *(early twentieth century).*

Above left and right: Zandra Rhodes, a fashion designer who typifies the seventies, makes colourful and flowing clothes of intricate design and beautiful workmanship.

Right: Bill Gibb's designs are in a similar vein, in as much as they appeal to the young and rich, who crave something more exotic than the uniform of trousers worn by most women of the early seventies.

Above: The ultimate in topless dressing, a painted-on bra over which a see-through blouse can be worn, photographed in Carnaby Street in 1968.

Above right: A fashion show staged by students from the Kingston Polytechnic, Surrey. The model wears hot-pants and a top of machine-made patchwork.

Below: A Bill Gibb fantasy dress. His ideas have been culled from the Renaissance and the Pre-Raphaelites.

little sign of a return to more formal wear. In the United States the cocktail dress survives. In England in particular (and among young people in general) fantastic and exotic evening clothes are often worn.

Alongside the growth of casual dressing (including Ruben Toress's collarless shirt for men that set a brief fad in roll-necked evening wear) other movements away from the mainstream of fashion have emerged. Nostalgia has been a recurring theme of our time, with designers raiding the twenties, thirties, forties and even fifties for inspiration. Young people, weary of ever-increasing standardization in clothes and fabrics,

have taken to buying old clothes. Flea markets, old army uniforms, sales of Hollywood wardrobes and even jumble sales have provided a small sector of youth with a wardrobe that baffles their elders and commercial moguls alike.

Among all the explicable and obvious fashions come the surprises. None is more puzzling than the reintroduction of the long skirt, abandoned with the world wars. Maxis were first seen during the late sixties, when calf-length and ankle-length skirts were promoted as the answer to the mini. The midi was swiftly engulfed by a wave of male disapproval but the ankle-length skirt has survived as everyday wear for a

small number of young western women. To see long skirts flowering and flourishing in a world of commuting by underground trains, jumbo jet travel and increasing urbanization is a charming and heartening example of the waywardness of women in how they choose to dress. It shows how fashion moves in cycles, constantly straining towards change yet always returning to the same themes.

What of the fashions of the future? Perhaps we shall find ourselves going further back in time, seeking a modern equivalent of the complicated embroideries of the Renaissance that made dresses into works of art. Zandra Rhodes, with her ephemeral, hand-painted, wispy gowns, has created wonderful otherworldly clothes that rely on body movements to gain their effect. At the more popular end of the fashion market are Indian cottons with machine embroideries in large eye-catching designs. What we still lack is something in between, clothes made by individual wearers for themselves and their friends, perhaps with embroideries or appliqué in a modern idiom; clothes that can achieve the status of an heirloom to be handed down the generations as we have inherited the beautiful hand-worked clothes of the Victorian era. As leisure time increases, with the possibility of the three-day weekend looming, perhaps this ideal will be realized.

Above right: The seventies' nostalgia for the twenties is curious, and is seen at its best in two outfits designed by the American Bill Blass. The outfits are complete with cloche hats.

Above far right: A Bill Blass evening dress with matching coat of clinging matte jersey, with a long fox boa draped round the neck.

Right: A third Bill Blass outfit of a pyjama suit for evening wear, showing the influence of Japanese Kabuki costume.

125

*This page: John Bates'
designs are more elegant, less
ephemeral, but still typical of
British couture fashion of the
seventies. Again, they show
the intricate workmanship
and design demanded by
couture buyers, but in a more
restrained manner.*

Bibliography

Adburgham, A., *Modes and Manners from Punch*, 1841-1940 (Hutchinson, 1961), *Shops and Shopping* (Allen and Unwin, 1964). Bell, Q., *On Human Finery* (Hogarth Press, 1947). Bergler, E., *Fashion and the Unconscious* (Brunner, 1952). Binder, P., *The Peacock's Tail* (Harrap, 1950). Burton, E., *The Georgians at Home* (Longman, 1967). Cunnington, C.W., *The Perfect Lady* (Max Parrish, 1946), *A Handbook of English Costume in the Eighteenth Century* (Faber and Faber, 1964), *English Women's Clothing in the Present Century* (Faber and Faber, 1952). Cunnington, C.W. and Cunnington, P., *A History of Underclothes* (Michael Joseph, 1951). Cunnington, P. and Mansfield, A., *English Costume for Sports* (A. and C. Black, 1969). Earl, A.M., *Costume in Colonial Times* (David Nutt, 1894), *Two Centuries of Costume in America*, 1600-1800 (David Nutt, 1905). Garland, M., *Fashion* (Penguin, 1962), *The Indecisive Decade* (Macdonald, 1968). Gummere, A., *The Quaker* (Ferris and Leach, 1901). Hartnell, N., *Royal Courts of Fashion* (Cassell, 1971). Hill, G., *A History of English Dress* (Bentley & Son, 1895). Laver, J., *Dandies* (Weidenfeld and Nicolson, 1968), *A Concise History of Costume* (Thames & Hudson, 1969). McClellan, E., *Historic Dress in America*, *1800-1870* (George Jacobs, 1910). Poiret, P., *My First Fifty Years* (Gollancz, 1951). Waugh, N., *The Cut of Men's Clothes, 1600-1900* (Faber and Faber, 1964). Wilkerson, M., *Clothes* (Batsford, 1970).

Index

Aken, Joseph Van 28
A-Line 41, *44, 45*
Allen, David 77
Aniline dye 32
Apron 22, 108
Art, Goût, Beauté 43
Art Nouveau 56
Artois, Comte d' 53, *53*
Austen, Jane 33, 52, 58
Aved, J. A. J. 55

Balenciaga, Cristobel 41, *116*
Ballin, Ada 72, 80
Balmain *44, 120*
Bandeau 80
Banyan 54, *100,* 101
Barbier, Georges *115*
Bascinet *19*
Bates, John *126*
Bathing costume *1*
Baudelaire, Charles 89
Bauhaus *53*
Beaton, Cecil *116*
Belcher, Jonathan 100
Belfast 70
Belgium 21
Belle Assemblée, La 105, 108
Béraud, Jean *43, 79*
Beret *41,* 53
Binder, Pearl 104
Blass, Bill *125*
Bloomer, Amelia Jenks 69, 70, 72
Bloomers 70, 72, 73, 79, 80, *109*
Blouse 36–37, 67, 80
Bodice 20–21, *64,* 77
Boiler suit *41*
Bonnet 52, 55, 77, *101, 105*
  Calash *107,* 108
  Poke 57
Boots 20, 21, 65, 88
  White 117
Bosse, Abraham 20, *21, 25*
Boulton, Matthew 54
Bra 116
Breeches 16, *20,* 25, 71
  Knee *67,* 77
  Riding 17
Brocade 27
Brummell, Beau 53, 85, 86, 88, *89,* 90
Buckram 20
Bulwer-Lytton 88–89
Burns, Robert 7
Burton, Sir Richard 75, 92
Bustle 27, 33, *33,* 36, 60–61, 72
Butterick 32
Button 53, *53, 63,* 88
Byron, Lord *89,* 90, 92
Byzantine *14*

Calico 104–5
Cane 56, *57*
Cap 22, 28, 48, 52–53
  Mob 52, *55, 104*
Cardin, Pierre 117

Carmignani, Giulio 58
Carmontelle, Louis de *31*
Carothers, W. H. 61
Carpaccio 7
Catherine of Braganza 24
Chamberlin, Joseph 96
Chandler, Winthrop *104*
Chanel, Coco 37, 54, *116,* 121
Chapman *63*
Charles I 21, *21*
Charles II 22, 24, *24*
Chase, William Merritt *102*
Chaucer 13
Chaworth, Lady 25
Chemise *40,* 41, 53, *53,* 59
Chesterfield, Lord 47
Chevalier, William 56
China 11
Chintz 27
Churchill, Randolph *92,* 96
Cleanliness 86, 88, 90
Clive 84
Clive, Mrs. Archer 60
Clouet *17*
Codpiece 16
Coffey, Charles 83
Commode 25
Copeley, John Singleton *100*
Corelli, Marie 72
Cossacks 68
Cotehardie *12, 19*
Courbet, Gustave 75
Courrèges, André 117
Cowl *12, 19*
Cramsie Family *1*
Crespine 12
Crèvecoeur, Chevalier de 104
Cricket 79–80
Crinoline 20, *32,* 33, *33,* 41, 60, 64, 72
Croquet dress 77

Dandy 83–97
David, Jacques-Louis *35,* 54
Dark Ages 12
Décolletage 36, 64
Delacroix *70*
Delany, Mrs. 28
Denim *108,* 109
Deveria, Achille *32, 39*
Dighton, Richard *85, 93*
Dinghen, Mrs. 17
Dinner jacket 76
Dior, Christian *40,* 41, *44, 45,* 61, *116, 117*
Directory 29
Disraeli, Benjamin *88,* 89
Ditchley 20
Dongen, Kees Van *123*
Donghi, Antonio *111*
Doublet 16, 20, *20,* 25
Downman, John *71*
Drainpipes 96
Dressing-gown *90,* 92
Drouais, Germain *51*
Duez, Ernest *33*
Duffel coat 104
Dungarees 108–9

Edward III 13
Edward VII *92,* 93
Elizabeth I 17, 20, *20,* 22

Ellesmere Manuscript 13, *13*
Empire line *101,* 107
England 13, 17, 21, 24–25, 31–33, 36–37, 49, 61, 67, 99, 100, 118, 124
English Gentlewoman 32
English Spy, The 88
Englishwoman's Domestic Magazine, The 32
Evelyn, John 24

Fabergé, Carl 53, *63*
Farthingale 20, *20,* 21, 24
Fichu 58
Fortuny 40
Fragonard 58, 59
France 13, 16–17, 20–21, *22,* 25, 28, 32, *35,* 64, 67, 89–90, 99, 104, 116
François I *17*
Franklin, Benjamin 104–5
Freeman, Mr. *73,* 76
Froissart's Chronicles 9, *22*
Fry, Elizabeth *105,* 108
Fur 13, 112
Fustian 13

Gainsborough, Thomas *28, 29,* 57
Garbo, Greta 51
Geoffrin, Madame 28
George III 83–84
George IV *85,* 86
Germany 13, 118
Gernreich, Rudi 112
Ghislandi, Vittore *90*
Gibb, Bill *123, 124*
Gillary, James *51*
Givenchy, Hubert de *120*
Glyn, Elinor 76
Gogram 100
Gorgeous Gussie 81
Greek drapery 7, *29,* 60
Green, Rupert Lycett 97
Gronow, Captain 68
Guerard 71
Gurney, Joseph John 107
Gwynne, Nell 24
Gym tunic 80

Hair 12, 21–22, 25, 27, 29, 36, *39,* 47–49, 51–52
Hair powder tax 49
Halter neckline 64
Harper's Bazaar 111
Hat 29, *35, 43,* 52, 52–53, 55, 58, 76, 107
  Bowler 57
  Cloche 36, *40, 43,* 52, *125*
  Pillbox *44*
  Top 93
  Tricorne *79*
Haute couture 116–18, 120
Hawes, Elizabeth 113
Haydon, Benjamin 89
Head-dress 12–13, *13, 18,* 25, *48,* 49
Heath, William *83, 86*
Hell's Angels 97
Hennin 12, *18*
Henry III 16–17
Henry VIII *16*
Hill, Hannah 108
Hilliard, Nicholas *22*
Hippies 97
Hogarth, William *48*

Holbein 16, *16*
Holland 21
Hollywood 112
Hoop 27, 29, 31, 60
Hose 16, *19, 21*
Hot pants 64, *65,* 76, *79, 124*
Hour glass *36*
Howe, Elias 33, *104*
Huxley, Aldous 53

Incroyable 84, *85*
Ingres 63, 67, *90*
Inspector 83
Isabella *18*
Italy 14, 21, 118

Jacket 17, 37, 76, 84, 93
Jaeger, Dr. 61
James, Charles *109*
Janssens, Hieronymus *1*
Japan 11, 120
Jeans 76, 81, *108,* 109
Jewelry 53–54, *63,* 84
  Costume 54
Jolly-Bellin 90
Junot, Laure 31

Khanh, Emmanuelle *65*
Kirtle *18*
Knickerbockers 69, 70
Ladies European Magazine 105
Lady's Realm 91
Landsknecht 16
Langberg, Jorn *117*
Lap dog 57, *58, 107*
Largillière, Nicholas *22, 58*
Lawrence, Thomas 35
Lenglen, Suzanne 80
Levi-Strauss *108,* 109
Lewes and Brighthelmstone Journal, The 57
Liberty, Lazenby 92–93
Lingerie 61
London Magazine 49, 101
Louis XIV *20,* 22, 24–25, 27
Lumbershirt 108
Luttrell Psalter 12, 19

Macaroni 84–85
Maclise, Daniel 88
Mainbocher 41, 112
Mallet, Jean-Baptiste 27
Man-made fibre 37, 116
Marble, Alice 80
Maria Theresa 8, 48
Marie Antoinette *8,* 28, *31,* 48
Mass production 37
Merveilleuse 84, *85*
Mill, John Stuart 67
Miniskirt 115, 117
Mitchell, Margaret 105
Moccasin 103
Mods 96–97
Monet, Claude 75
Montagu, Edward Wortley 48
Monuel, Bouette de *33*

Napoleon 29, 31
Nash, Ogden 76
Nattier *83*
New Look *40,* 41, 61, 116

Newman 81
Nylon 61

Orsay, Alfred d' *88*, 89
Osterberg, Bergman 80
Oxford bags 69

Page-boy cut 52
Paniers 27
Pantaloons 67–70, 88
Paper dress 64
Paquin 37, *118*
Parasol *32*, 36, *56*, 57, *75*, *102*
Patchwork *101*, 103, *124*
Patou 80, *119*
Peg-tops 69
Pelisse *101*
Périn, Lis-Louis *31*
Periwig 25
Peruke 25
Petticoat 17, 27, *28*, 33, 41, 59–61
Phillips, Thomas 89
Picasso, Pablo *111*
Pisañ, Christina de *18*
Plus-fours 69
Plutarch 12
Poiret *118*
Pompadour, Madame de 28, *31*
Port Folio 105
Poulaines 14
Pre-Raphaelite *47*
Prudhon, Pierre 88
Punch 58, 60, *64*, *73*, 93, *109*
Purefoy, Henry 48, 83
Pyjamas 75–76

Quaker dress 107
Quant, Mary *45*, 115–17, *121*

Raeburn, Sir Henry 76

Rational Dress Campaign 49, 61, *69*, 70, 72
107
Ready-to-wear 33, *65*, 117–18, 120
Red Indian 103
Redgrave, Richard *39*
Reed, Richi *45*
Reichenau *14*
Reynolds, Sir Joshua *48*
Rhodes, Zandra *123*, 125
Ricci, Nina *120*
Richlieu, Cardinal 21
Riding-dress *39*
Robespierre *90*
Rockers 97
Romance of the Rose, The *18*, *19*
Rome *64*
Rossetti, Dante Gabriel *47*
Rousseau 56
Ruff 17, *20*, 21

Sack 116
Sackcloth 13
Sackville, Richard *21*
Saint Laurent, Yves 117, *121*
Sassoon, Vidal *51*
Satin 13, 20
Savile Row 89
Seurat, Georges *56*, 57
Sewing machine 33
Sexual display 59, 63–64
Shawl 53, *58*, *105*, 108
Shift 36–37, 75
Shirt 67, 93
  Open-neck 90
Shoes 14, *19*, *44*, 79
Shorts *80*
  Bermuda 113
Silk 20, 27, *40*

Singer, Isaac 33
Skinhead *96*, 97
Skirt 21, *76*, 77, 124–25
Slacks 76
Slashing 14, 16
Sleeve 13, 16, *18*, *28*, 31, *32*, *37*, 40, 47
  Leg-of-mutton 107
Smock 81
Smollett 63
Spain 17, 20
Speed, John *9*, *20*
Srackowes 14
Starching 17
Stephen, John 117
Stockings 61, 67
Stocking tights 115
Stripes 85, *86*, *90*
Stubbes, Philip 20
Sun-expelling mask 102
Svinin, Pavel Petrovich *107*
Switzerland 67

Tailored suit *43*, 67
Tartan 68–69
Teddy boy 96
Templer 12, *12*
Thimonnier, Barthélemy 33
Times, The 60
Tissot, James 68
Topless fashion 64, 112, 115, *124*
Tour, Quentin de la *31*
Town and Country Magazine 84
Train 33
Trousers 67–81, 93
Turban *90*, *100*, 101
Tweed 69
Twiggy 79
Tyrian purple 12

Umbrella 56–57
Underclothing 59–61
Unisex 79, 81, 121
United States 32–33, 36–37, 49, 53, 61, 67,
  77, 81, 99–113, 116, 120, 124
Utility clothing 37

Velvet 13, 16, 83, 89, 92
Vinyl 116
Vionnet, Mme 37, 109
Virgil 12
Vogue 111
Voisard *47*
Voltaire 56

Waistcoat 77
Walking suit *36*
Walpole, Horace 48
Washington, George 47, 53, 86, 99, 102,
  104–5
Watteau de Lille 55
Watteau pleat 27
Wellington, Duke of 56
Whistler, James McNeil 99
Wig 48, *48*, 101
Wilde, Oscar 89, 93, 109
Winklepickers 96
Winterhalter, Franz Xavier *39*
Winthrop, Fitz-John 100
Wollstonecraft, Mary 67
Women's Liberation Movement 65, 81, 115,
  121
Women's Wear Daily 111
Worth, Charles Frederick 60, *116*

Zip 115

Acknowledgments

The author and publishers would like to thank the following organizations and
individuals for supplying illustrations for this book:

Reproduced by gracious permission of Her Majesty the Queen: title page;
Abby Aldrich Rockefeller Folk Art Collection: 103, 107;
Ardea Photographics: 86 top;
Bassano & Vandyke: 36 right;
John Bates: jacket front, 126, back endpaper;
Rodney Bennett: 97 top;
Bildarchiv Foto Marburg: 27;
Bill Blass: 125;
Bodleian Library: 18 bottom, 19 bottom;
Clive Boursnell: 123;
British Museum: jacket back, p. 7, 9, 10, 11, 12 top, 13 bottom, 16 bottom, 18 top,
  19 top, 20 top, 22 top, 35 bottom, 51 top right, 53 bottom, 56, 82, 86 bottom;
Brooklyn Museum: 101 bottom;
Bulloz: 26, 29 bottom, 30, 31 right, 32 top, 33 top & bottom, 34 38, 39, 42, 48 bottom
  right, 53 centre, 54, 55 top & bottom, 62, 63 top left, 66, 67, 70, 71 bottom, 74, 75,
  78, 87, 90 right;
Camera Press: 44 top left, 45, 52 bottom, 57 bottom right, 64 bottom, 65 top right,
  79 left, 96 top & bottom, 97 bottom, 116 left, 120 top left & right, 121 top;
Central Press Photos: 80;
Collection Viollet: 41 top, 53 top, 84 bottom;
Cooper-Bridgeman Library: 4-5, 43 bottom, 63 top right (London Museum), 71 top,
  118 top;
Culver Pictures Inc: 99, 104 top, 113;
Daily Telegraph Colour Library: 79 right;
Mary Evans Picture Library: 92 right;
Fox Photos: 65 bottom, 73 bottom, 81 left, 117 top centre & right, 121 bottom left,
  centre & right, 124 top left & right;
J. R. Freeman: 60, 105 top;
Freer Gallery: 98;
Giraudon: 58, 59 top, 88 bottom, 91;
Harvard University Portrait Collection: 100 right;
Hirmer Fotoarchiv Munich: 14, 15;
Illustrated Newspapers Group: 49 bottom, 69 bottom, 115;

Jaeger: 61;
Keystone Press Agency: 120 bottom;
Kodak Museum: half title, 113;
Library of Congress: 49 top;
Mansell Collection: 8;
Marshall & Snelgrove: 40 bottom right;
Metropolitan Museum of Art, Rogers Fund: 106;
National Gallery, London: 35 top left;
National Gallery, Scotland: 29 top, 90 left;
National Gallery, Washington: 100 left, 104 bottom;
National Portrait Gallery: front flap, 22 bottom, 23, 48 top, 50, 85 top left; 88 top left;
Phaidon: 57 (Art Institute of Chicago);
Popperfoto: 44 bottom;
Private Collection: 16, 17;
Punch: 64 top, 73 left, 109 top;
Radio Times Hulton Picture Library: 24, 32 bottom, 37 bottom, 40 bottom left,
  41 bottom, 47, 48 bottom left, 65 top left, 68 top, 69 top, 72, 73 top right, 83, 84 top,
  89, 105 bottom, 112, 117 bottom, 120 centre top;
Royal Academy of Arts: 28 (Iveagh Bequest), 57 top, 68 bottom, 77 top;
Vidal Sassoon: 51 bottom; Scala: 6, 110, 111, 122;
Snark International: 35 top right, 43 top right, 51 top left, 90 left, 102, 114;
South Sea Bubble: 81 bottom;
Levi Strauss: 108;
Paul Tanqueray: 65 centre top;
Tate Gallery: 28 bottom, 29;
The Times: 124 bottom;
Union Française des Arts et du Costume: 43 left, 118 bottom, 119, back flap;
Victoria & Albert Museum: front endpaper, 12 bottom, 13 top, 17 top & right,
  20 bottom, 21 top & bottom, 25, 36 left, 39 top, 40 top left & right, 94-5, 101 top,
  109 bottom;
Wallace Collection: 59 bottom:
Wartski: 63 bottom.